BEYOND WHITE PRIVILEGE

In the world of academic anti-racism, the idea of white privilege has become the dominant paradigm for understanding racial inequality. Its roots can be traced to radical critiques of racial capitalism, however its contemporary employment tends to be class-blind, ignoring the rifts that separate educated, socially mobile elites from struggling working-class communities.

How did this come to be? *Beyond White Privilege* traces the path by which an idea with radical potential got 'hijacked' by a liberal anti-racism that sees individual prejudice as racism's primary manifestation, and white moral transformation as its appropriate remedy. This 'politics of privilege' proves woefully inadequate to the enduring forms of racial and economic injustice shaping the world today. For educated white elites, privilege recognition has become a ritual of purification distinguishing them from their working-class counterparts. For the white working class, whose privileges have eroded, but not disappeared, the politics of privilege often looks like class scapegoating – a process that has helped to drive increasing numbers of alienated whites into the arms of white nationalist movements.

This book offers an alternative path: an 'interest convergence' approach that recaptures the radical potential of white privilege discourse by emphasizing converging, cross-racial interests – in education, housing, climate justice, and others – that reveal that the 'racial bribe' of whiteness is ultimately contrary to the interests of working-class whites. It will therefore appeal to readers across the social sciences and humanities with interests in issues of racial inequality and social justice.

Andrew J. Pierce is Associate Professor of Philosophy and Director of Justice Studies at Saint Mary's College in Notre Dame, IN. He earned his Ph.D. in philosophy from Loyola University Chicago, specializing in social and political philosophy broadly conceived, with interests in critical theory and the philosophy of race. He is the author of several articles in these areas, as well as the book *Collective Identity, Oppression, and the Right to Self-Ascription*.

Routledge Research in Race and Ethnicity

BEYOND WHITE PRIVILEGE

How the Politics of Privilege Hijacked Anti-Racism

Andrew J. Pierce

Routledge
Taylor & Francis Group

LONDON AND NEW YORK

Designed cover image: Getty

First published 2024
by Routledge
4 Park Square, Milton Park, Abingdon, Oxon OX14 4RN

and by Routledge
605 Third Avenue, New York, NY 10158

Routledge is an imprint of the Taylor & Francis Group, an informa business

British Library Cataloguing-in-Publication Data
A catalogue record for this book is available from the British Library

ISBN: 978-1-032-60945-4 (hbk)
ISBN: 978-1-032-60943-0 (pbk)
ISBN: 978-1-003-46121-0 (ebk)

DOI: 10.4324/9781003461210

Typeset in Sabon
by SPi Technologies India Pvt Ltd (Straive)

CONTENTS

ACKNOWLEDGEMENTS

This book owes a debt of gratitude to a number of individuals and organizations. Some of the ideas developed here were presented and workshopped at conferences organized by the California Roundtable on Philosophy and Race, the American Association of Philosophy Teachers, the Philosophy of the City Research Group, the Great Lakes Philosophy Conference, and Indiana Campus Compact. Colleagues who have provided valuable feedback on the core ideas of the book include Megan Zwart, Bettina Spencer, Lisa Pruitt, Ranjan Rohatgi, Michael Monahan, David Ingram, Charles Mills, Ronald Sundstrom, Alonso Villaran, Gordon Purves, Kathleen Turner-Purves, Michael Ventimiglia, Ken Knies, Steven Michaels, Brian Stiltner, Jesse Bailey, Carisa Cortez, Colleen Butler-Sweet, and Amanda Moras. I am grateful to the acquaintances, friends, and family members, too numerous to mention, with whom I have had conversations about these topics over the years. Your insights and perspectives are greatly valued. Finally, I am deeply indebted to my partner, Wendy Pierce, for insightful discussions, but more importantly, for the kind of love and support that makes this or any complex human endeavor possible.

INTRODUCTION

The Walk of Shame

Picture a typical classroom. The desks have been dragged away, leaving only the twenty-by-twenty-foot space, filled with about twenty college students standing in a side-by-side line stretching from one wall to another. The students are a diverse group, roughly half from a two-year college in a mid-sized Rust Belt city, the other half from a selective liberal arts college in the same region. Both groups are racially diverse, though the two-year college students tend to be more diverse in age and less economically diverse than the other group. Almost all of them describe themselves as working class. The liberal arts students include a couple of international students. Both groups include several first- and second-generation immigrants, mostly from Central America.

The line of students divides the front and back half of the room, like an equator. Once everyone is settled (a bit anxiously, having not yet received any indication of the purpose of the exercise), the game begins. A facilitator asks the students a number of questions:

If your ancestors were forced to come to the U.S., not by choice, take a step back.

If your relatives or ancestors' land was forcibly made part of the U.S., take a step back.

If you had a parent who inherited wealth, take a step forward.

If at least one parent earned a master's or Ph.D., take a step forward.

DOI: 10.4324/9781003461210-1

The questions continue, becoming increasingly personal:

If you've ever had to skip a meal or were hungry because there was not enough money to buy food, step back.
If you were raised in a two-parent household, step forward.
If you were ever afraid or were the victim of violence because of your race, class, ethnicity, gender, or sexual orientation, step back.

At this point, the facilitator notices some students becoming increasingly uncomfortable. Their slight, unconscious bodily movements, followed by hesitation to move in one direction or the other, lead the instructor to suspect that some of them may be withholding painful personal experiences. Still, a pattern is emerging, with most students of color, along with a disproportionate number of the two-year college students, falling toward the back of the room, and most of the white students moving toward the front.

A few more questions move beyond personal experience to solicit judgments about American culture:

If your school textbooks positively reflected your racial or ethnic identity, step forward.
If you saw your racial or ethnic group portrayed in degrading roles on television, step back.

After a few more questions of this nature, it becomes clear that the facilitator should have chosen a bigger room. The white students at the front of the classroom have run out of space to move forward, taking small, uncomfortable steps in response to questions that apply to them. They take advantage of the exercise's geography to avoid looking backward at their less advantaged classmates.

Similarly, the mostly Black and brown students at the rear of the classroom have found themselves with their backs pressed firmly against the wall.[1] Yet they can clearly see the patterns that have emerged in front of their eyes. An older Black woman is visibly holding back tears and abruptly leaves the room.

The exercise ends, and now it's time for reflection. The students are reluctant at first, but eventually have much to say. One of the few white students near the back, a corrections officer in a local prison, takes his position in the classroom as evidence that class, rather than race, determines one's place in American society. This prompts one of the few students of color who ended up near the front, a Nigerian-American woman who stepped forward when the group was asked whether they grew up in a home with servants, to admit that she doesn't really understand claims about systemic racism. She suspects that many of the racial inequalities in the U.S. have more to do with the attitudes of Black Americans than with racism and offers her own immigrant family's success as evidence for this view. An expensively dressed Latina student from the back of the room echoes this view, and two students of color voicing this perspective leads several white students to chime in and agree. One adds that Black people can be racist too, prompting nods of agreement from several other students, including the older Black woman who left the classroom and has returned apologetic and a bit embarrassed. The corrections officer shares some of the colorful racial epithets directed at him by inmates: honkey, cracker, and so on. The facilitator carefully redirects, avoiding any further cataloging of racial slurs, and presses gently but critically on the responses thus far, seeking to push the students' reactions beyond kneejerk and into the rarefied realm of "difficult conversations," the navigation of which might be extolled in tenure files and grant applications.

A Black student near the back has been quiet up to now, but his face reveals a simmering mixture of frustration and sadness, with the exercise itself or the reality it reflects or both. Now he speaks up. Black attitudes, he explains, are not responsible for the fact that the average white family controls nearly ten times the wealth of the average Black family and is twice as likely to own their own home; nor that Black folks are three times as likely to be killed by police compared with whites and five times as likely to be incarcerated; nor that Covid-19 hospitalization and death rates are significantly higher for Black Americans than for white Americans; nor that American schools and neighborhoods continue to be segregated by race half a century after *Brown vs. Board of Education*. This is a student who appears to be acutely aware of the current realities of racial inequality in the U.S., even if his focus on Black–white inequality conceals the experiences of non-Black people of color to some degree.

A purple-haired white student wearing a shirt that reads "abolition is the future" eagerly agrees with the Black student's presentation of these facts, nodding her head vigorously and adding a few more statistics of her own. But beyond this, the introduction of statistics into the conversation sends a chill through the room. The facilitator tries to revive the discussion, reliably, by asking how the exercise made the students feel. The group offers a complex mix of emotions: guilt, sadness, anger, and helplessness. One white student who ended up near the front shares that she feels grateful for everything her parents did to provide her with these unearned advantages.

The facilitator notices that time is running short, and brings the discussion to a close by thanking students for their vulnerability and acknowledging the elusiveness of racial equality while assuring the group that their efforts today represent a step in the right direction.

* * *

Most of us who have been involved in anti-racist work in educational, activist, or other contexts have encountered some version of this exercise, usually called a "privilege walk." I myself have facilitated or participated in close to a dozen such exercises. The above account is pieced together from a number of real, and in my experience typical, reactions.

There is almost always at least one participant of color who is brought to tears, as the traumas of racial inequality are manifested in a highly visible form. There is always some defensiveness and frequently some anger among white students, who resent the implication of racial privilege and deflect by insisting on the struggles their own ancestors overcame or by redirecting the conversation toward the prejudices of people of color. There are usually a few white students eager to announce their privilege and, to my initial surprise, often one or two who express a kind of gratitude for it, utterly misunderstanding the point of the exercise. There are usually a few class-based exceptions to the pattern of racial inequality that emerges, which can provide another opportunity for deflection though occasionally lead to interesting discussions about the connections between race and class.

The particular distribution of these responses varies by context. The exercise proceeds differently, for example, in a selective liberal arts college in the Northeast compared with a public university in the American South. It also looks different as part of a corporate diversity training program rather than a college course. But in all of these contexts, white strategies of resistance are visible in varying degrees, and the racial trauma of Black and other people of color is instrumentalized for the sake of the presumed growth and learning of white participants.

These flaws, however, are not unique to the design of this particular exercise. Sociologist Leslie Margolin describes similar, if less creative, exercises, including one where facilitators "seat white students in circles … and ask them to write down how membership in the majority race makes their lives easier, then, one by one, read those privileges out loud to one another and the group as a whole."[2] Another exercise has participants rotate among different stations, each containing a number of statements associated with a particular kind of privilege (race privilege, gender privilege, ability privilege, and so on). The participants then attach beads to a string for each description that applies to them, creating a physical representation of their accumulated privileges.

These practices and exercises instantiate a particular approach to antiracism, an approach I call "privilege politics" (or, in its specifically educational uses, "privilege pedagogy"). At bottom, privilege politics and pedagogy aim to increase awareness of racial inequality by encouraging white people to recognize the various ways that their racial status provides them with unearned advantages relative to people of color. In this respect, it is essentially a theory of racial inequality, well grounded in empirical evidence, as we shall see. But one of the main shortcomings of the approach, as I will strive to demonstrate, is that despite its popularity, privilege politics provides no real path to action or change. That is, it is often unclear what its subjects are supposed to do with their newly unearthed awareness of their privilege. The purveyors of privilege politics speak of "dismantling," "betraying," or "relinquishing" privilege, of using it for good, or simply of working for racial equality, committing to racial justice, and so on. But these vague prescriptions inevitably lack detail, and because the step from privilege awareness to racial justice is often obscure, the recognition of privilege tends to become an end in itself – an exercise in individual moral purification rather than social transformation. As a result, while the exercise often leaves a strong impression on its participants, its effectiveness as a tool for racial justice is extremely limited.

In spite of this ineffectiveness (or perhaps, on a more cynical view, because of it), privilege politics has become widely influential in educational settings, in corporate diversity programming and public relations, in celebrity "activism" and more. The approach has been so successful that in certain domains, the acknowledgement of one's privilege has effectively become a precondition for engaging in discussions of racial justice, akin, perhaps, to the role of admitting you have a problem in various twelve-step programs. It has also developed an unearned reputation for being a radical or progressive alternative to moderate, liberal approaches to anti-racism, ignoring the enthusiasm with which much of corporate America has adopted its language and rituals.

In fact, by equating anti-racism with white self-reflection and psychological transformation, contemporary privilege politics reveals itself as the descendent of a liberal anti-racism that sees individual prejudice as racism's primary manifestation, and white moral conversion as its appropriate remedy. Whether or not this was an effective approach to anti-racism in the pre-civil rights era, it is surely inadequate in the present, when racism is more likely to manifest in race-neutral policies and institutions with disparate impact than in prejudice-driven acts of racial discrimination.

Thus, the task of this book is twofold, having both a critical and a constructive component. The critical component presents an indictment of privilege politics, based on both historical and psychological evidence. I argue that, while privilege politics originated in radical analyses of racial capitalism, it is eventually co-opted and neutralized by liberal discourses in a process the philosopher Olufemi Taiwo calls "elite capture." The result is a sanitized, class-blind concept that fails to understand or effectively challenge racial injustice.

In addition to this historical analysis, I provide a critical analysis grounded in social psychology, one which identifies the ways in which the privilege-based approach flies in the face of powerful cognitive biases and patterns of thinking. Asking white Americans to acknowledge their racial privilege requires them to concede that their successes and accomplishments (and those of their families) are largely the result of luck and unjust favoritism while recognizing that the obstacles and challenges faced by people of color are vestiges of injustice, for which they are largely not responsible. While perhaps accurate, this sort of realization is precluded by a well-established category of cognitive biases called *attribution biases*. Attribution biases incline us to draw just the opposite kinds of conclusions: that our own accomplishments are the result of our hard work and effort, and our challenges and shortcomings the result of external factors for which we are not responsible. As for others, we are inclined to view their successes with suspicion and interpret the obstacles they face as the result of individual flaws and failures. Even worse for privilege politics, biased attributions of this sort are easily generalized to the level of groups, extending favorable attributions to those I perceive to be like me and unfavorable attributions to those that I perceive to be different.

This critique of privilege politics, presented in both historical and psychological terms, is developed in Chapters 1 and 2, respectively. In Chapter 3, I draw on both components of the critique to explain how privilege politics has shaped the contemporary political landscape. I show that the proliferation of privilege politics, which entails a kind of class-based scapegoating, has managed to alienate large numbers of working-class whites and has thus contributed to the rise of Trumpism and extreme nationalism, the resurgence of neo-fascist movements, the reactionary attack on (what is often mislabeled as) "critical race theory," and more. I am not sympathetic to these developments; however, understanding how privilege politics has turned working-class white communities away from racial and economic justice efforts is crucial to bolstering effective resistance to them, beyond empty condemnations. Considering the history and current demographics of the U.S., a movement for racial and economic justice that fails to secure the support of the white working class is unlikely to succeed.

This insight leads me to the constructive component of the book, in which I develop an alternative to privilege politics, an approach to racial and economic justice I call an "interest convergence" approach. This alternative, which I describe in Chapter 4, has its roots in the work of critical race theorists like Derrick Bell, who argued that racial progress tends to occur only when it coincides with the interests of whites. Bell's analysis of the civil rights movement – and especially the movement toward desegregation grounded in the *Brown v. Board of Education* decision – held that these developments were the result not of an intrinsic trajectory toward racial justice, nor of a fundamental shift in white public morality, but rather of a historical moment in which the domestic racial policy of the United States was undermining its Cold War pretensions to be the liberationist alternative to Soviet communism. Insofar as this image was crucial to U.S. national interests, a measure of equality was granted to Black Americans that had until then been withheld, as it would not have benefitted whites to grant it. In Bell's view, then, it was this convergence of Black and white interests that explains the much-celebrated advances of the civil rights era.

Critical race theory, and Bell's work especially, is frequently associated with a deep skepticism about racial progress (Bell refers to such skepticism as "racial realism"). Thus, its employment of interest convergence typically appears in service of deflationary interpretations of what look to many like transformational moments in U.S. racial history. But the theory is not without its own implications for pursuing racial justice. Once one abandons the politically naïve view that racial justice comes about primarily through the moral transformation of previously immoral institutions or individuals, one can refocus on identifying, articulating, and expanding areas of overlapping interest among whites and people of color. Unlike the contemporary politics of privilege, this politics of interest convergence retains the potential for radical social transformation in the interest of racial and economic justice.

Chapter 5 explores what this approach would look like in a number of specific contexts: education, housing policy, environmental justice, and more. But it also makes the broader case that what makes the politics of interest convergence truly radical is its potential to reorganize the lines of solidarity and political affiliation to effectively resist what scholars and activists have come to call racial capitalism. Racial capitalism describes an economic system that targets populations of color for special, extreme exploitation. But to pretend that such a system, which has brought humanity to the brink of social and ecological collapse in pursuit of profit, advantages white communities in any ultimate sense, is to miss a crucial point. The economic forces that drove European colonization, produced the transatlantic slave trade, and now sustain mass incarceration are the same forces that have deindustrialized, offshored, and drugged rural white communities into social disarray. Ultimately, resistance to racial capitalism is the ground on which broad, cross-racial interests must be identified and pursued.

To make this point is not to return to the bad old days of color-blind class reductionism. That capitalism lurks underneath many forms of racial exploitation does not mean that ignoring race in favor of class is the right path forward. Rather, what the new theorists of racial capitalism offer is a genuinely intersectional account (another conceptual innovation of critical race theory) that pays attention to the ways in which racial oppression works on and through class differentiation and economic exploitation. A politics grounded in this sort of framework has the potential to do more than just encourage white self-reflection and moral improvement. It has the potential to connect Black and brown radical traditions with a renewed white progressivism grounded in the interests of working-class whites.

Rejecting the individualistic moralizing of privilege politics does not mean that morality is wholly irrelevant to anti-racist pursuits, however. In the sixth and final chapter, I explore the complex relationship between morality and social change, drawing on a rich history of philosophical reflection addressing this relationship. Utilizing both classical and contemporary forms of virtue ethics, I argue that the moral psychology of individuals and the justice of social institutions are mutually constitutive. While this does entail the possibility of shifts in morality driving social transformation, it also recognizes the opposite sort of causality, where social and institutional change causes shifts in moral thinking. The insight supports a pluralistic approach to anti-racism, engaging in campaigns of persuasion where appropriate and working for institutional change directly where this is a more promising path to justice. I show, finally, how the politics of privilege fails to appreciate this mutual constitution, focusing on moral persuasion and posturing regardless of its efficacy.

Moving beyond privilege politics is the first step toward a broad, interracial coalition for racial and economic justice. For a nation (and a world) that is increasingly polarized and rapidly descending into fascism and authoritarianism, it may be the only path forward, not just toward racial and economic justice but for our very survival as a species. I hope that the following pages make some small contribution to understanding how to move forward along this path.

Notes

1 In this book, I follow the revised (2020) Associated Press style guide, which recommends the capitalization of 'Black' as a racial designation, but not 'white,' 'brown,' or other color-based racial designations. While this practice may seem somewhat inconsistent, it presumably relies on a judgment about the moral asymmetry of dominant and subjugated racial identities (at least in the case of 'white' versus 'Black'). See the AP statement here: https://blog.ap.org/announcements/the-decision-to-capitalize-black#:~:text=AP's%20style%20is%20now%20to,a%20color%2C%20not%20a%20person.

2 Leslie Margolin, "Unpacking the Invisible Knapsack: The Invention of White Privilege Pedagogy," *Cogent Social Sciences*, 1.1 (2015): 1053183.

1

THE PATH OF PRIVILEGE

The idea of white privilege, if not the term itself, is often traced back to a fascinating passage near the end of W. E. B. Du Bois' masterful early twentieth-century work, *Black Reconstruction*. In the context of an analysis of how "the doctrine of racial separation…overthrew Reconstruction by uniting the planter and the poor white," Du Bois describes the social advantages offered to white workers in lieu of actual monetary compensation. The passage is worth quoting at length.

> It must be remembered that the white group of laborers, while they received a low wage, were compensated in part by a sort of public and psychological wage. They were given public deference and titles of courtesy because they were white. They were admitted freely with all classes of white people to public functions, public parks, and the best schools. The police were drawn from their ranks, and the courts, dependent upon their votes, treated them with such leniency as to encourage lawlessness. Their vote selected public officials, and while this had small effect upon the economic situation, it had great effect upon their personal treatment and the deference shown them. White schoolhouses were the best in the community, and conspicuously placed, and they cost anywhere from twice to ten times as much per capita as the colored schools. The newspapers specialized on news that flattered the poor whites and almost utterly ignored the Negro except in crime and ridicule.[1]

This remarkable passage not only anticipates the key features of racial inequality that would roil American society for the next hundred years, it suggests that these features are part of an intentional strategy, a "carefully

DOI: 10.4324/9781003461210-2

planned and slowly evolved method" aiming to undermine the unification of Black and white workers. By rewarding racial solidarity among whites, the plantation class simultaneously discouraged class unification, thereby securing a powerful form of social control. Such a strategy can explain much about race relations through the twentieth century and into the present. Du Bois' claim that "there probably are not today in the world two groups of workers with practically identical interests who hate and fear each other so deeply and persistently and who are kept so far apart that neither sees anything of common interest" might overlook some significant differences in the life experiences of Black and white Americans today, but, as we shall see, it also captures substantial commonalities between the experience of working-class whites and working-class people of color.

The idea that the function of racism is to divide the population continues to be popular enough to risk becoming cliché. Worse, it is often cleverly misused not just to condemn racism itself but to condemn any kind of discourse that might draw attention to its existence. This is an especially common view among the white working class, and it often grounds the assumption that the appropriate response to racism is to ignore it, to become "color-blind" in both personal and political pursuits. I will analyze the abuse of this idea in some detail, as it is key to understanding the liberal neutralization of Du Bois' radical analysis. But for now, let us simply note the essential function of white privilege: to undermine class unity and thus protect race- and class-based exploitation alike. It is precisely the awareness of this function that disappears from many contemporary accounts of white privilege.

Du Bois' account of the "wages of whiteness" provided a sturdy foundation for a generation of white radicals rethinking the relationship of race and class in the turbulent 1960s and '70s. Du Bois' influence was frequently noted, for example, by author and activist Theodore Allen, whose concept of "white skin privilege" likely marks the first use of the term. Allen was a working-class scholar who developed Du Bois' idea into a full-blown labor history, produced, ostensibly, in his spare time between jobs as a factory worker, a coal miner, a postman, a librarian, a teacher, and more. Allen argued that, as the description of his monumental study *The Invention of the White Race* puts it, "when the first Africans arrived in Virginia in 1619, there were no white people there." That is, he argued that whiteness emerged as a "ruling class racial formation," a social category capable of placating working-class whites by uniting them with plantation and industrial elites rather than similarly situated workers of color.[2]

Beyond the two opposing classes invoked by traditional Marxist analysis, Allen argued that this white racial formation represented an "intermediate stratum," which served to secure white racial solidarity over interracial class solidarity. By implementing a system of social privilege that allegedly derived from the racial superiority of white workers, white elites were able to gain their loyalty and prevent the sort of interracial labor unrest exemplified by Bacon's Rebellion, which Allen identifies as the main catalyst for the "invention" of whiteness. Thus, "white skin privilege" served a stabilizing function, one which became a source of pride for the Southern plantation class, who noted the relative stability of chattel slavery as a form of social control, especially compared with the riotous class conflicts of European societies at the time. Despite various economic disadvantages imposed by the plantation system (not least of which was the challenge of competing with "free" slave labor), Southern white workers could eventually be relied upon to defend the system of slavery, along with the system of white skin privilege to which it was connected. One might call this the *stabilizing function* of white skin privilege.

Allen compares this function to similar strategies of colonial domination in Mexico and Peru, where Spanish authorities conferred certain powers and privileges upon an existing intermediate class of native *caciques*, thus securing their loyalty and grooming them to help ensure social control in the colonies. Conversely, Allen attributes the challenges of British subjugation of the Irish as well as Portuguese colonization of Brazil to the *lack* of an available intermediate stratum. These latter cases, however, provide the exception to the general rule of colonial domination: that effective social control and economic exploitation require the development of an intermediate class consisting of a socially privileged group nonetheless lacking in ultimate political and economic power. To this analysis, one might add any number of further examples, from Rwandan ethnic divisions nurtured by Belgian colonial powers to the intermediate class of "coloured" South Africans. That these divisions are often the source of inter-ethnic strife in postcolonial societies demonstrates that they are a continuation of colonial violence rather than a remnant of uncivilized tribalism, as former colonial powers are often inclined to see them. Moreover, the lingering potential for violence points us to another important feature of intermediary racial formations.

In addition to its stabilizing function, the formation of an "intermediate stratum" provides another advantage for maintaining social control. By dividing the working class along racial lines, when discontent arises among workers, this strategy allows for that discontent to be redirected and neutralized in the form of racial resentment. That is, blame for social and economic problems can be attributed to either the intermediate stratum or the racial underclass. This kind of scapegoating is the reverse side of racial solidarity. Critical theorists Theodor Adorno and Max Horkheimer, whom I discuss in Chapter 3, note the centrality of this kind of scapegoating in the development of European anti-Semitism, arguing that the racialization of the Jewish population served to "conceal domination in production" and thereby stabilized the fragile form of capitalism that was struggling to maintain itself in the unsteady decades between two world wars. Here, we can clearly see how the creation of an "intermediate stratum" not only serves to shore up racial loy-alty but also provides a ready outlet for oppositional energy: a dangerous release valve easily ramped up to genocidal extremes. We can call this the *scapegoating function* of racial formations.

Racial scapegoating of this sort is easily found wherever race- and class-based exploitation is rampant. In the United States, as the fragile protections of the New Deal began to crumble under the weight of neoliberal assault, white resistance to the destruction of a hard-won social safety net was neu-tralized by presenting it as the undeserved spoils of Black "welfare queens." Similarly, as economic globalization drives down wages and makes previ-ously secure white communities precarious, these communities are encour-aged to blame immigrant labor rather than the powerful forces of global capital. Here again, comparable economic interests are trumped by racialized narratives about threats to "our" way of life.

This sort of racial scapegoating is often noted in both academic and politi-cal modes of anti-racism. The possibility that intermediary groups could themselves be the target of scapegoating efforts is less appreciated and, in the case of working-class whites, more controversial. Class scapegoating, how-ever, is central to the critique of privilege politics that I develop in the pages that follow. For now, I am satisfied to identify two distinct, though comple-mentary ways that racialization serves to protect class- and race-based exploitation: stabilizing forms of social control through hierarchy and neu-tralizing dissent through scapegoating.

The intermediate stratum of whiteness also serves as a mechanism of inte-grating (some) immigrants in ways that do not fundamentally challenge white supremacy and racial capitalism. Alongside Allen's compelling analysis, fel-low activists and historians like David Roediger and Noel Ignatiev produced equally erudite studies of the process by which European immigrants previ-ously considered racially inferior to the English came to be included under the umbrella of whiteness. Ignatiev's *How the Irish Became White* is the clas-sic example, tracing the path by which a people deeply committed to libera-tion, and equally deeply opposed to slavery, came to support the "peculiar institution" through the bribe of white skin privilege.[3] Similarly, Roediger's *Wages of Whiteness* traces this history with a greater emphasis on labor and how the norms and imperatives of wage labor supplanted the Republican ideals of the early United States.[4]

As one can see even in this brief overview, a thorough understanding of the history of racial oppression and economic exploitation is critical to a clear-eyed view of white privilege. But let us also take care not to lose in the com-plexities of history the key point of the "wages of whiteness" argument: that white skin privilege is a Faustian bargain, a proximate advantage gained by sacrificing ultimate advantage. That is, from this perspective, white skin privilege is *not in the interest of the majority of whites*. To think otherwise is, as Ignatiev cleverly describes it, "equivalent to suggesting that swallowing the worm with the hook in it is in the interests of the fish."[5] This makes the rejection of white privilege not a selfless moral act of "allyship" but a self-interested, liberation-seeking political act. This distinction more or less captures the difference between liberal and radical approaches to the understanding of whiteness, and it will be central to the "interest convergence" approach to anti-racism that I describe in later chapters.

But first, it is necessary to trace the devolution of the white skin privilege doctrine – its dehistoricization, depoliticization, and capture by a class-blind form of liberalism inadequate to the task of social transformation.

* * *

Despite the history just described, it is increasingly common to trace the emergence of contemporary white privilege discourse not to Du Bois' "wages of whiteness" or Allen's "white skin privilege" but to Peggy McIntosh's short, seminal article "White Privilege: Unpacking the Invisible Knapsack." McIntosh describes white privilege as "an invisible package of unearned assets," which she proceeds, as the title suggests, to "unpack" and lay bare for critical reflection. These privileges include issues of cultural representation ("I can turn on the television or open the front page of the paper and see people of my race widely represented" and "I can be sure that my children will be given curricular materials that testify to the existence of their race"), physical and social mobility ("If I should need to move, I can be pretty sure of renting or purchasing housing in an area which I can afford and in which I would want to live" and "I can go shopping alone most of the time, pretty well assured that I will not be followed or harassed"), discrimination ("If a traffic cop pulls me over or if the IRS audits my tax return, I can be sure I haven't been singled out because of my race"), commercial convenience ("I can choose blemish cover or bandages in 'flesh' color and have them more or less match my skin"), and more. Such privileges, she claims, can be taken for granted most of the time by most white people, but not by most people of color.[6]

A feminist educator, McIntosh arrives at this list by extrapolating from gender-based privilege to race privilege. While men (and white people) may be increasingly open to the claim that women (and people of color) are disadvantaged, they are less amenable, she claims, to the idea that men (and white people) are "over-privileged." This marks the first significant difference between McIntosh's account and its precedents described above. For her, racial advantage and disadvantage constitute a zero-sum game, and a proper understanding of racial oppression entails "seeing [one]self as an oppressor, as an unfairly advantaged person." There is no sense in her self-reflective analysis that this sort of advantage might be proximate or self-defeating. Nor, despite her insistence that race and other forms of oppression are "interlocking," is there any sense that race privilege might serve a stabilizing function, that the passively "advantaged" and the intentional "oppressors" might not be identical. This is likely because McIntosh's analysis is largely ahistorical, employing a meditative mode of personal reflection that Asad Haider has described as "the reduction of politics to the psychology of the self."[7]

In fairness, McIntosh's article does encourage its readers to move beyond the traditional liberal view that equates racism with individual prejudice and focus instead on "redesign[ing] social systems" and "reconstruct[ing] power systems on a broader base." This might lead one to believe that her conception is in fact undergirded by some kind of transformational politics. But neither the article nor her subsequent reflections on white privilege specify these vague recommendations in any meaningful way. Rather, her analysis moves not from a moral critique of explicit prejudice to a political critique of white supremacy (presumably the "system" she has in mind, though she doesn't identify it as such) but rather from a critique of explicit prejudice to a critique of *implicit* or unconscious prejudice (or, perhaps, ignorance, ambivalence, etc.). In specifying her demand to "redesign social systems," for example, she warns that "we need first to acknowledge their colossal unseen dimensions. The silences and denials surrounding privilege," she says, "are the key political tool here."[8]

This reveals another of the essential features of white privilege discourse: a focus on the passive, unconscious acceptance of advantage, distinct from the active, intentional forms of discrimination that the term "racism" more typically connotes. Privilege pedagogues like McIntosh aim to challenge the idea that only "racists" in the traditional sense are responsible for racial injustice, and place the onus more broadly on those who benefit from racial injustice, regardless of their beliefs or attitudes about members of other races. This emphasis on subconscious assumptions and attitudes about race links privilege discourse to other trends in academic anti-racism, including those emphasizing implicit bias, microaggressions, and other semi-conscious manifestations of prejudice. But acknowledging the subconscious dimensions of racial bias, important as it might be, does not constitute a politics, nor does it transcend the liberal assumption that the key to racial justice lies in the transformation of white people rather than the transformation of sociopolitical structures. Rather, the "political" task of privilege politics and pedagogy becomes simply to "raise awareness" of such biases, with little reflection on how (or whether) this awareness might lead to action.

I characterize this view as 'liberal' primarily in the philosophical sense. While the average American is likely to think of 'liberal' as synonymous with a left-wing political orientation, philosophical liberalism is a rather different thing. Philosophical liberalism emerged as an Enlightenment-era challenge to monarchical political power and the authoritarian and hierarchical structures that undergirded it. For liberals, individual freedom is paramount, and any legitimate political power must derive its authority from the free consent of those it purports to govern. From this basis, liberals derive a specific conception of democracy, *liberal* democracy, where the freedom of citizens is embodied in certain basic rights and expressed democratically through the choice of political representatives. However, equally important to the liberal worldview is the fundamental right to property and the alleged independence of economic power from political control: the so-called "free market." That is, the freedoms that liberals conceive as inalienable typically include the "freedom" of workers to sell their wages to employers, free from the meddling influence of the state, and the corresponding freedom of employers to reap the rewards of this relationship. For this reason, liberals like John Locke are often considered the intellectual founders not only of liberal democracy but also of modern capitalism.

Much more could be said about philosophical liberalism, but this brief summary suffices to introduce the idea of liberal anti-racism. Since liberals see political and economic power as fundamentally distinct, their visions of social reform tend to be relegated to a narrow "public sphere," where a variety of moral and political worldviews compete in a "marketplace" of ideas. Here, citizens can attempt to persuade each other of, among other things, the right courses of political action and the proper modes of moral conduct. But while the former might find some uptake through formal political channels, the latter necessarily remains private (or, at most, semi-public), as liberals insist that the State remain neutral among competing moral worldviews. This is most clearly expressed in the liberalism of John Stuart Mill, who insists not only on the neutrality of the State but on complete freedom of speech in the public sphere, where even the most noxious views are allowed expression, if only to provide citizens with the benefit of "the clearer perception and livelier impression of truth produced by its collision with error."[9]

Within liberal parameters then, anti-racism appears primarily as a moral discourse competing for allegiance in the public sphere (presumably with any number of racist worldviews), attempting to convince an allegedly rational and open-minded public of, at various historical moments, the wrongness of slavery, the injustice of Jim Crow, or the irrationality of racial prejudice. Moreover, for liberals, racial prejudice is understood as the root cause of racial injustice. So, the path to social change necessarily goes through the white psyche. If whites can be persuaded to overcome their racial prejudice, then presumably the systems rooted in such prejudice can thereby be transformed.

In addition to being psychologically naïve (Mill's assumptions that "there is on the whole a preponderance among mankind of rational opinions and rational conduct" and that "wrong opinions and practices gradually yield to fact and argument" certainly require an explicit defense in our age of conspiracy and irrationality), this sort of view fails to appreciate the extent to which racial prejudice can be the effect of racial injustice as much as its cause (a possibility I discuss further in the final chapter). This is precisely the causal analysis that underlies the "wages of whiteness" analysis. If it is correct, even in part, a focus on white racial prejudice, explicit or implicit, will inevitably fail to address the root causes of racial and economic injustice.

* * *

The ineffectiveness of McIntosh's ahistorical "politics" of privilege is reason enough to seek alternative approaches. But this critique rather underestimates the dangers of privilege politics. Beyond its ineffectiveness, one can argue that privilege politics actually sustains racial injustice, not only by neutralizing critical energy (and thus, ironically, performing the very stabilizing function that white skin privilege arose to perform) but also by contributing to the radicalization of whites who refuse to confess and renounce their racial privilege. That is, as some critics have already pointed out, white privilege discourse may be less about white psychological transformation than about white moral redemption, a redemption that relies on a certain kind of intraracial class scapegoating. As Leslie Margolin puts it, "the knowledge whites gain from unpacking their invisible knapsacks allows them not only to retain their imagined innocence and moral elevation, it allows them to retain the very privileges they claim to be renouncing." He continues:

> This discourse may be less about changing an unjust system than it is about freeing those who operate that system to think of themselves as innocent, egalitarian, and antiracist... Insofar as white privilege confessors define themselves as non-oppressive and antiracist, as far better than ordinary whites, they can continue to reap the rewards of ordinary whites without serious damage to their self-image. They can even act as if it is their responsibility to show others the way. They can insist that their antiracist views should be acknowledged and celebrated, and that future conversations about race and racism should be organized around their own anxieties, opinions, and struggles. Above all, they can imagine that the world wants to know, in minute detail, what it means to have been born white in America, as if speaking about their whiteness marks them off, to a certain extent, as heroic, as if sharing the details of their whiteness and privileges somehow undermines the old order—anticipates the coming revolution.[10]

Here, we must ask an important if uncomfortable question: who are the purveyors of this moralizing discourse, and who are the "ordinary whites" from whom they seek to distinguish themselves?

Shannon Sullivan provides a plausible answer in her insightful book *Good White People: The Problem with Middle Class Anti-Racism*. Sullivan argues that intra-racial class biases are "one of the central ways by which middle-class white people avoid taking responsibility for and fighting against white privilege."[11] By portraying poor and working-class whites as the *real* racists, "middle-class" whites are able to establish their own moral goodness by contrast, dispelling their racial guilt and recapturing their racial innocence. Sullivan carefully reconstructs the "race-class etiquette" that sustains the distinction between "good" whites (which she frequently equates with being "liberal," though in the more familiar political sense rather than the philosophical sense described above) and their race-class others: "white trash," "hillbillies," "rednecks," and the like. By "cleansing" whiteness of these undesirable elements, white liberals maintain their moral purity and cleverly redirect responsibility for racial injustice. Sullivan notes the ineffectiveness of such performative anti-racism, noting that it is not so much "an attempt to eliminate racial injustice... but a desire to be recognized as Not Racist."[12]

It's not hard to see the rituals of privilege politics as part of this race-class etiquette, with an ironic twist. Here, the way to mark oneself as a "good" white person is to acknowledge one's complicity, one's undeserved advantage, one's "badness." Simply to catalog and describe one's racial privileges, as McIntosh notes, "makes one newly accountable." That is, it puts one on the path to moral redemption. The *real* racists, of course, are those who refuse such accountability, who refuse to acknowledge their racial privilege. *They* remain mired in unconscious bias, in ignorance, in complicity. Thus, the central task of anti-racism, once we have confessed our own racial sins, is to evangelize to our fellow sinners, those whites whose "silences and denials" still allegedly uphold the pillars of white supremacy.

The evangelical language of sin and salvation is hard to avoid here. Just as in past eras religious orders inserted themselves into social hierarchies between the peasantry and the powerful, today a growing cadre of Diversity, Equity, and Inclusion (DEI) officers, cultural competency consultants, racial sensitivity trainers, and other educated elites has arisen to disseminate and administer this system of race-class etiquette. This is not to deny that many of the folks in these positions are deeply, non-performatively committed to racial justice, nor that good work gets done under the DEI banner. But when CoreCivic, the United States' largest operator of private, for-profit prisons, has a Vice President of Diversity, Equity, and Inclusion, it's clear that the forces of racial capitalism have largely co-opted whatever critical potential this upwardly mobile class of social managers might have initially wielded.[13]

This process of appropriation is likely to be familiar to those working for structural change or even to anyone familiar with the histories of countercultural resistance to systems of entrenched power. There are few more effective ways of neutralizing resistance than appropriating and institutionalizing it in a watered-down, symbolic form. Olufemi Taiwo's conception of "elite capture" helps us understand this sort of appropriation and, more specifically, the process by which the idea of white privilege is deradicalized and "captured" by liberal discourses.

Taiwo describes elite capture as a process by which "the advantaged few steer resources and institutions that could serve many toward their own narrower interests and aims."[14] He uses the idea primarily to develop a nuanced position on "identity politics," a phenomenon, he argues, with a trajectory of appropriation similar to the one I have described above. At its outset, identity politics sought radical structural change, soliciting broad-based support and solidarity for a political movement that did not reproduce the racist, sexist, and homophobic tendencies of the system it aimed to transform. Taiwo argues that, as it became increasingly embedded in academic institutions, however, the movement was largely captured by elites, devolving into a sectarian "politics of deference" that replaced intergroup solidarity with deference to select representatives of marginalized groups. The result, he concludes, is a "fragmentation of political collectivity" that seriously undermines the possibility of collective action capable of real systemic change. In Taiwo's view, this makes the captured version of identity politics "ultimately anti-political," though he insists that this is a condemnation not of identity politics as such but rather of the process of elite capture that co-opts it.

I contend that we can understand the capture of privilege politics in much the same way that Taiwo understands the capture of identity politics. This would probably not surprise Taiwo, since he observes that "almost everything in our social world has a tendency to fall prey to elite capture."[15] As the politics of privilege migrates from the radical periphery to the center of academic institutions, its practitioners increasingly obscure its distinctive intersectional class-consciousness until it finally disappears from sight. This is hardly a coincidence, as educational institutions (especially colleges and universities) are centrally involved in managing and reproducing hierarchies of class. Whether this sort of distortion of the discourse is intended or not is beside the point. As Taiwo points out, elite capture is a kind of "system behavior," involving "an observable (predictable) pattern of actions involving individuals, groups, and subgroups, each of whom may be pursuing any number of different goals from their own narrow point of view."[16] So whether the class-blindness of privilege politics emerges from the psychological blind spots of its authors, the complex bureaucracies of educational institutions, the influence of external benefactors, or something else entirely, it is nonetheless observable, and its political implications can be effectively analyzed without getting too caught up in the motives of individual actors. With this in mind, let us return to Sullivan's analysis, which insightfully emphasizes the role of intra-racial, class-based scapegoating in privilege politics.

For all of the promise of Sullivan's account, she unfortunately does not fully avoid the pseudo-religious character of white privilege discourse, nor the "reduction of politics to a psychology of the self" that it entails. Perhaps this is because she has also defined white privilege ahistorically, as a "constellation of psychical and somatic habits formed through transaction with a racist world."[17] Perhaps it is because her answer to white scapegoating is not a political but a "spiritual" transformation of whiteness. What white people need, she claims, is "to become spiritually healthy enough that they do not poison other races when interacting with them but instead reciprocally nourish each other," to "adorn their souls with genuine treasures, rather than the counterfeit gems of white supremacy."[18]

Poetic though it might be, the emotional rehabilitation of white people marks an underwhelming conclusion to a powerful analysis of the way that anti-racist discourse falters upon intra-racial scapegoating. While it may be true that white supremacy involves affective and perhaps even "spiritual" harm to whites, nurturing whites' psychological and emotional health is unlikely to lead to structural transformation in the interest of racial justice. To imagine otherwise is to assume the familiar causality of liberal thinking, conceiving of white psychological malaise (if not prejudice, on Sullivan's view) as a cause, not an effect, of systemic injustice.

To her credit, Sullivan does consider Ignatiev's call to "betray" and "abolish" whiteness. But her swift rejection of this view seems to misunderstand its political and historical character. Sullivan includes an analysis of the "betrayal" of whiteness enacted by the "race traitor" alongside allegedly comparable emotions of guilt and shame. While she acknowledges that "betrayal also is an event or an act, not just an emotion," her analysis largely treats it as the latter, due to its having "a significant affective component associated with losing trust and feeling tricked or misused."[19] Accordingly, Sullivan laments that betrayal lacks a "positive valence," and thereby confesses that "I do not have much confidence in the positive effects of building an identity exclusively on destruction, nor do I think that asking people to conceive of themselves as treacherous destroyers is likely to be a fruitful recruiting device in most cases."[20]

Sullivan also contends that the call to "betray" or "abolish" whiteness "operates with insidious class/race hierarchies." Allegedly, this is because the call is "not equally welcoming of lower-class white people and white trash in particular."[21] This is attributed to the fact that "betrayal" requires secure belonging in the first place, and lower-class whites lack this stable belonging in whiteness. Owing to this, Sullivan concludes that the "race traitor's act of betrayal is essentially an act of class privilege."[22] And yet, in the same paragraph, she notes that "if we want to retain the language of abolition, we ought to recognize that merely existing as white trash already opens up the possibility of white abolition, because it already troubles the stability and meaning of whiteness."

Such a critique seems to wholly miss the class character of Ignatiev's analysis. That working-class whites are ideally positioned to undertake a betrayal of whiteness, that their privileged status is unstable, is not lost on Ignatiev and his Marxist colleagues. Indeed, it is the entire point of the analysis of white skin privilege, which, notwithstanding other noteworthy differences that have emerged among white Americans since, was initially extended *precisely* to working-class whites, to secure their allegiance to a white elite. While it is fair to note that today such calls tend to come from the privileged halls of academic institutions rather than shop room floors, to level this kind of critique against Ignatiev and his colleagues is to misunderstand their analysis, dismiss their own personal histories as working-class scholars, and, most importantly, conceal the history and genealogy of white skin privilege and the "wages of whiteness."

Sullivan's critique of the alleged class privilege of white abolitionists, as well as her concern for the "negative valence" of the language of betrayal make sense only within a highly individualistic worldview. If one imagines the "betrayal" of whiteness as an individual act, performed, perhaps, within the confines of a classroom or on the virtual stage of social media, one can easily see it as a virtue signaling act of class privilege or as entailing a negative and isolating set of implications about one's individual identity. But race and class are not, primarily, individual identities. "Betraying" whiteness does not mean refusing to check the 'white' box on your college application, nor does it mean publicly declaring one's non-whiteness (perhaps in the way that *The Office's* Michael Scott "declared" bankruptcy). It means working together with others to transform systems that harm whites and people of color alike (albeit the latter often more concretely and the former more indirectly). And whenever one is working together with others, the possibility of developing positive, self-affirming identities is at least latent.

Similarly, though Sullivan is right that white identity is not something that white people can simply cast off like an ill-fitting garment, this image also betrays a liberal individualist's understanding of what it means to abolish whiteness. For Ignatiev, Roediger, Allen, and others, just as the "invention" of whiteness was a collective, political act, so its undoing must be. They are not advocating for Rachel Dolezal-esque rejections of whiteness, nor a superficial "I identify as a human being" variety of color-blind humanism. They are encouraging white people to reject the bribe of white skin privilege, to recognize the ways in which their well-being is bound up with that of their Black and brown compatriots, and finally, to *act* on that awareness in ways that undermine the specific operations of white supremacy in our daily lives. The goal is precisely to overturn "insidious class/race hierarchies," not to reproduce them, as privilege politics does.

* * *

What I have attempted to trace here is a history of the idea of white privilege, emphasizing its capture and transformation by a liberal discourse that conceals the true nature of white supremacy. By sleight of hand or short-sightedness, the new theorists of white privilege have erased the inextricable link between white supremacy and racial capitalism, the stabilizing role of white skin privilege, and, above all, the truth that such privilege is *not* ultimately in the interest of the majority of white people. In its place, they offer a liberal view of white psychic reprogramming: a turn inward rather than outward, reflective of the steady transformation of political activity into therapeutic discourses of self-care. But what the world needs now is not more white introspection. What the world needs now is action: collective action across lines of race, class, and other forms of difference, motivated by carefully and inclusively articulated common interests (and perhaps also, we must admit, by the identification of common enemies).

This is not to say that psychology is irrelevant to a proper understanding of white privilege, nor to appreciating how anti-racist and other social justice movements have failed to achieve their goals. In fact, it is a question of moral psychology that perhaps marks the biggest challenge for liberal theories of white privilege, like McIntosh's. If white privilege provides unearned and unqualified advantages to white people, what incentive would they have to reject it? Why seek to undermine a system that benefits you? Insofar as the new theorists of white privilege can provide a coherent answer to this question, they typically concede that privilege is ultimately *not* in white people's interest.

For example, Frances Kendall, who describes herself as a "Consultant for Organizational Change Specializing in Issues of Diversity and White Privilege," acknowledges the "personal and public costs of maintaining racism and the systematic supremacy of whiteness," adding that "even if we know we have privilege, we are usually only clear about what we gain from being white, not what it costs us."[23] Similarly, the philosopher Paula Rothenberg, wondering what would motivate a white person to voluntarily relinquish white privilege, surmises that

> Beyond questions of justice are matters of self-interest. History tells us that in the end, an unjust and inequitable distribution of resources and opportunities leads to terrible violence. Increasingly, wealthy white people in America find themselves living in gated communities as they seek ways to protect their lives and their property, and people of all racial/ethnic backgrounds and every economic class complain of feeling unsafe on the streets and in their homes. A society that distributes educational opportunities, housing, health care, food, even kindness, based on the color of people's skin and other arbitrary variables cannot guarantee the safety of its people. In this sense, all of us, both the victims and the beneficiaries of racism pay a terrible price.[24]

This insight forms the core of what I will call an "interest convergence" approach to anti-racism, an approach that begins by identifying the ways in which white supremacy and racial capitalism undermine the interests of white folks as well as people of color, rather than by cataloging the multitude of proximate advantages that whiteness offers. Such an approach stands a much greater chance of winning the crucial allegiance of the white working class than the currently prevalent methods, many of which are grounded in a superficial, ahistorical understanding of white privilege. To better understand why, we will need to pursue a more nuanced, psychologically informed explanation of why many white students and citizens alike are alienated by privilege politics. In the next chapter, I explore some of the deep-seated cognitive biases that undermine privilege politics, and I provide a more detailed analysis of why the "psychological wage" of whiteness is such an effective strategy in the first place. In this way, we can continue to develop our inquiry into more effective modes of anti-racist politics with the benefit of a solid empirical foundation in social psychology.

Notes

1 W.E.B. Du Bois, *Black Reconstruction in America: An Essay toward a History of the Part Which Black Folk Played in the Attempt to Reconstruct Democracy in America, 1860–1880* (New York: Oxford University Press, 2007): 700–701.
2 Theodore Allen, *The Invention of the White Race. Vol. I. Racial Oppression and Social Control* (London: Verso, 1994).
3 Noel Ignatiev. *How the Irish Became White* (New York: Routledge, 1995).
4 David Roediger, *The Wages of Whiteness: Race and the Making of the American Working Class*. 4th ed. (London: Verso, 2022).
5 The quote comes from a pamphlet written as an intervention in the tumultuous 1969 National Convention of *Students for a Democratic Society*, entitled "Without a Science of Navigation We Cannot Sail in Stormy Seas." It can be found at the Marxist Internet Archive here: https://www.marxists.org/history/erol/ncm-1/debate-sds/ignatin.htm.
6 Peggy McIntosh, "White Privilege: Unpacking the Invisible Knapsack," *Independent School*, 49.2. (1990): 31–35.
7 Asad Haider, *Mistaken Identity: Race and Class in the Age of Trump* (London: Verso, 2018): 46.
8 McIntosh, "White Privilege," 35.
9 John Stuart Mill, *On Liberty* (Kitchener, ON: Batoche Books, 2001): 19.
10 Margolin, "Unpacking the Invisible Knapsack."
11 Shannon Sullivan, *Good White People: The Problem with Middle Class Anti-Racism* (Albany: SUNY Press, 2014): 5.
12 Ibid.
13 The evolution of DEI work, and its grounding in a liberal, diversity-based framework of social reform will be discussed in greater detail in the final chapter.
14 Olufemi Taiwo, *Elite Capture: How the Powerful Took Over Identity Politics (And Everything Else)* (Chicago: Haymarket Books, 2022): 22.
15 Ibid.
16 Ibid, 10.

17 Shannon Sullivan, *Revealing Whiteness: The Unconscious Habits of Racial Privilege* (Bloomington, IN: Indiana University Press, 2006): 63.

18 Ibid, 168.

19 Sullivan, *Good White People*, 138.

20 Ibid, 139–140.

21 Ibid, 141.

22 Ibid, 142.

23 Frances E. Kendall, *Understanding White Privilege: Creating Pathways to Authentic Relationships Across Race*. 2nd ed. (New York: Routledge, 2013): 23.

24 Paula S. Rothenberg, *White Privilege: Readings on the Other Side of Racism*. 5th ed. (New York: Worth Publishers, 2016): 5.

2

BUILDING A WALL

Psychological Barriers to the Effectiveness of Privilege Pedagogy and Politics

Teaching about race in predominantly white schools provides an illuminating glimpse into the ways in which privilege politics provokes white resistance, both in the classroom and in society at large. Conversely, finding effective ways to teach on the topic of race to white students may have promising implications for transformational politics. In this chapter, I explore the psychological barriers that limit the effectiveness of privilege-based approaches in both pedagogical and political contexts. Despite its pretense to reveal and reform the white psyche, privilege-based accounts like McIntosh's are rarely grounded in solid empirical science. By contrast, an understanding of key psychological biases like attribution bias, just world bias, and others reveals the shortcomings of privilege politics and will help us construct an alternative that avoids activating them in unproductive ways.

Anecdotal accounts of the resistance of white students abound in discussions of privilege pedagogy. Kirsten T. Edwards, for example, recounts the challenges of discussing white privilege in the classroom as a woman of color:

> White students, particularly White men, seemed to resent me. Sometimes they would just sit in their seats scowling, refusing to participate in the class discussion. No matter how much I worked to create an equitable environment, a safe space where we could thoughtfully engage these ideas, some of my students adamantly refused.[1]

Kathy Glass describes other strategies of white resistance:

> Some [white students] attempt to deny their relation to whiteness as a site of privilege, citing their working-class background. Others point to the

DOI: 10.4324/9781003461210-3

hard work that has allowed them and their families to advance in life without government assistance or social preference of any kind. Some may resent the implication that they have done otherwise, and believe they are being exposed to far-left dogma in the classroom.[2]

Similarly, A. Todd Franklin notes white students' "reticence to truly reconcile themselves to the social ramifications of their whiteness,"[3] and Maria del Guadalupe Davidson calls whites' inability to come to terms with their own privilege a "significant pedagogical problem."[4] Kevin Lally's book-length study *Whiteness and Anti-Racism*, focused on his experience teaching mostly white high school students, describes feeling "stuck" within the framework of white privilege pedagogy:

> In a dynamic familiar to many teachers who do classroom work with race, very few if any students "converted"… Most came into my room having encountered some kind of antiracist pedagogy, typically McIntosh's invisible knapsack, and had their opinions of White privilege ready to hand. The students who accepted the antiracist framework of White privilege, those who identified as White allies especially, nodded along to classroom activities detailing racism and were vocal in small and large group conversations. They reinforced my lesson plans and occasionally provided additional stories or information to strengthen the case for the existence of racial inequality. Yet those students typically brought their views with them…Our exchanges felt like a rehearsal, like a scripted dialogue we parroted to each other.

Of the more skeptical white students, Lally writes:

> The students who resisted played an essential role of object to be acted upon and converted. When they shared arguments or concerns, I listened so that I might recognize and rebut them. And while some students pushed back out loud, most students stayed quiet during these exchanges… I got the sense that most students simply waited these units out, hoping to avoid saying the wrong thing.[5]

If one of the key purposes of education is to encourage students to critically examine (and possibly change) their views and assumptions about the world, privilege pedagogy seems to be failing in this respect. As explored in the previous chapter, liberal students often approach the topic as an opportunity to verify their credentials as "good" whites and to distinguish themselves from their "bad" white peers. On the other hand, conservative and working-class white students, if they are not vocally resistant to these lessons, are increasingly learning (and being instructed) to engage in a kind of resistance by disengagement. Everyone goes through the motions and ends up in the same place they began, some more convinced of their moral superiority vis-à-vis their peers, and some more convinced of (or at least amenable to) conservative critiques of the alleged left-wing bias of educational institutions.

Such an approach fails to push liberal students from an abstract commitment to anti-racism to a concrete understanding of acting for social change. And perhaps even more concerning, it all but delivers conservative and working-class white students to the reactionary racist forces that claim to provide a supportive space where they need not self-censor. (Ominously, Lally lists among the white students reticent to privilege pedagogy those who "spend too much time in the darker corners of the internet," the same darker corners that have produced a wave of white supremacist terrorism in recent years.) These students need to be empowered not only to understand our complex racial history but to see themselves as having a positive role to play in it. In both political and pedagogical endeavors, their agency must be respected, and they must be recognized as partners and collaborators, not as objects to be acted upon by beneficent liberals. The failure to approach the white working class (especially) in this way has contributed significantly to the dangerous political situation the United States now finds itself in, as I will explain in the next chapter.

But first, if we really want to understand how to empower students and fellow citizens alike, we need to develop a more nuanced understanding of the nature of psychological responses to white privilege discourse. Why do white responses tend to cluster around either moral posturing or self-serving denial? As we will see, both responses derive from the same psychological need: the need to maintain dignity and secure social recognition. But denial especially is illuminated by an understanding of the common biases that are activated when thinking about responsibility, blame, and social (in)justice.

* * *

Imagine yourself alone in your car, driving home on a dark winter evening. Not one of those postcard-perfect, bleach-white snow evenings, but a wet, gray midwestern February, where everything seems to be covered in a frozen slush the color of dirty dishwater. The roads are slick, but nothing you haven't seen before. You drive the few miles in the kind of semiconscious state familiar to the regular commuter. Low-volume talk radio provides an unremarkable soundtrack to the day's gray monotony. You're not really listening – that is, until a few words catch your attention (something about white privilege, perhaps?). At this, you briefly look to the console to turn up the volume. When your eyes return to the road, bright red brake lights have illuminated your windshield. You apply your own brakes, but it's too late. You slide through the icy slush for only a moment before crunching into the rear end of the car in front of you. Thankfully, the accident is not too serious. Your crumpled front fender has absorbed most of the damage, and neither you nor the other driver has been noticeably hurt. The question that your mind now turns to is: who is responsible?

I don't mean legally responsible. In general, the rear-ender is usually legally responsible in rear-end collisions. I don't even mean to engage in an analysis of moral responsibility, in any deep philosophical sense. What I want to consider, in order to illuminate a certain kind of psychological bias, is how you, as the rear-ending driver, are likely to *feel* about who is responsible. There are various factors to consider. Yes, you looked away for a moment to turn up the radio, which might suggest that you are at fault. But also, the weather is objectively horrible, and, hey, who put a stop sign just around that bend in the road anyway, only visible at the last moment? And the driver in front of you must have really jammed on the brakes herself. You don't even recall seeing her in front of you before the accident. These external factors provide ample opportunities for you to deflect at least some of the blame for the accident. After all, you are generally a good driver. Not the type to cause accidents.

This sort of blame deflection reflects a broad category of cognitive bias called attribution bias. Attribution bias has to do with how we explain human actions and their outcomes, both our own and those of others. More specifically, it has to do with whether we attribute behaviors to intrinsic, personality-based factors or extrinsic, situational factors. Attribution bias is displayed both in differences in the way we explain positive and negative behaviors and in the discrepancy between how we explain the behavior of others compared with our own. In the above scenario, for example, even if you ultimately take responsibility for the accident, acknowledging your momentary distraction, you are likely to note some external factors too: bad weather, a poorly placed stop sign, and so on. In the absence of other factors (e.g., unusually low self-esteem), you are not likely to draw from the incident any conclusions about your *internal* character: that, for example, you are a bad driver or an easily distracted person.

On the other hand, our psychological tendencies are precisely reversed when explaining positive behaviors (or, to put it another way, successes rather than failures). If I am awarded a competitive grant or if I make the basketball team, I am likely to attribute my success to intrinsic factors: talent, dedication, hard work, and so on. I am not likely to look very hard for external factors to explain my success.

If, however, someone else is chosen over me, I will typically be much more inclined to look for factors extrinsic to that person to explain their success: their grant proposal must have been "trendy," the player's family must be friends with the coach, and so on. In short, we are psychologically inclined to understand our successes as deserved, reflective of internal characteristics of our personality, while seeing our failures as accidental, a matter of simple bad luck. When judging others, however, our inclinations invert, and we leap easily from individual misfortunes to negative judgments about personal character. Likewise, we readily dismiss the success of others as undeserved, proceeding from external factors rather than internal ones. This imbalance in how we judge ourselves versus others is sometimes called "self-serving bias," for obvious reasons.

Already, one can begin to see how "self-serving" attribution bias works against privilege politics, an approach that asks white students and citizens to accept explanations of social facts that are precise inversions of the kinds of explanations they are psychologically inclined to accept. It asks them to understand negative outcomes for people of color not as personal failings (as they are psychologically inclined to do) but as the result of external social forces of injustice. This is a challenging enough task, for reasons I will discuss below. But even if white students can overcome attribution bias in order to recognize the causal force of racial injustice, white privilege discourse then asks of them something even more difficult. It asks them to understand their own "successes" primarily as the result *not* of their intrinsic hard work and effort but of an external (in their view, at least) fact about themselves: their categorization as white. As privilege pedagogue Frances Kendall puts it, "privileges are bestowed on us solely because of our race by the institutions with which we interact, not because we deserve them as individuals."[6] This makes it especially clear that privilege politics requires its adherents to see their advantages as derived from external factors rather than anything internal to their character.

Understanding attribution bias helps us understand whites' resistance to seeing themselves as recipients of this sort of privilege. The forms that such resistance frequently takes – insisting on hard work and effort as the true source of advantage; insisting that they themselves, or their family, or their European ethnic group has also faced unjust external barriers to success; relying on alternative explanations of injustice that evoke the personal shortcomings of people of color; and even transforming privilege acceptance into a mark of personal moral fortitude – are predictable given the nature of attribution bias.

The relevance of attribution bias is even more compelling when we consider that the bias that individuals display toward themselves is readily generalized to the level of groups. Just as I am more likely to accept or offer more forgiving explanations for my own behavior compared with that of others, I am more likely to accept or offer more forgiving explanations for the behavior of those I perceive to be *like* me, compared with those that I perceive to be different. Let's imagine another scenario here.

Imagine that you are walking down the street in a large U.S. city. Shamefully, just about any city you choose will have a significant number of persons lacking adequate housing, some of whom panhandle on the city's streets. Imagine that, as you walk down the street, one of these persons asks you for change. If you have lived in a larger city for any length of time, it's likely that you have developed some more-or-less automatic response to such encounters. Perhaps you systematically ignore such requests. Perhaps you politely decline and keep walking. Perhaps you always keep some spare money on hand to give. Let's try to get underneath these predetermined responses and think about the judgments we make about the people who find themselves in these situations. After all, our automatic responses are probably shaped by these judgments in some way.

It stands to reason that those who feel that unhoused individuals are victims of external forces of social injustice, marginalization, or simple bad luck are probably more inclined to hand over some cash, while those who see homelessness as evidence of personal failing are probably less inclined to offer help. Research on attribution bias tells us that judgements like these are shaped by our perception of whether the person we encounter is similar to or different from us: that is, whether or not we share a group identity or membership. If I am a military veteran, and I encounter another veteran experiencing homelessness, attribution bias suggests that I will be more likely to see this person as an undeserving victim of external forces rather than a deserving victim of personal failings. Similarly, if I am white, and I encounter an unhoused white person, attribution bias predicts that I will be more likely to think that this person's situation was a matter of bad luck or unfair treatment rather than bad choices, laziness, or personal vices. On the other hand, if I am white and the unhoused person is Black, attribution bias suggests that I am more likely to explain his homelessness in precisely the opposite way, as a result of personal failings, poor choices, and the like.[7]

This sort of generalized attribution bias, referred to by social psychologists as "in-group bias," is even more directly relevant to understanding resistance to privilege politics, which asks its target white audience to view both themselves and those racially like them as beneficiaries of undeserved privileges while accepting a more forgiving explanation of the situation of those who are racially different. Interestingly, while the original research presented attribution bias as a general psychological phenomenon, more recent research has suggested that the phenomenon is more prevalent among whites in Western societies and less prevalent in more collectivist societies and among non-white populations.[8] This makes privilege politics an especially poor approach for targeting precisely the populations most inclined to resist its assumptions.

* * *

Attribution bias points to the psychological need to maintain a positive image of oneself and the groups to which one belongs. It is thus closely related to "system justification" and "belief in a just world" (BJW) bias, which have been the focus of a large and interesting body of research perhaps even more directly relevant to privilege politics.[9] This research tells us that, for a variety of reasons, individuals have a deep psychological need to believe that the world is just and well-ordered. According to Melvin Lerner, the progenitor of the theory, belief in a just world renders the world manageable and predictable, which is "central to the ability to engage in long-term goal-directed activity."[10] But beyond being simply predictable, a just world is also one in which people get what they deserve. This belief thus mitigates the distress of being susceptible to harm by forces outside of one's control. If one just does what one is supposed to do, one need not worry about being subject to the winds of chance or the machinations of oppressive systems (which, of course, are not truly oppressive if they are deserved).

Belief in a just world thus motivates individuals to reinterpret situations or events that might be taken as evidence of injustice. This creates a significant barrier to understanding the experience of oppressed groups (and, obviously, of social injustice generally). One of the most common and pernicious manifestations of this bias is what psychologists call "victim derogation." Confronted with innocent victims of injustice (or even simple bad luck), observers tend to reinterpret their fate as being deserved – as resulting from character flaws, poor choices, bad behavior, and so on.[11] In one of the earliest demonstrations of this effect, Lerner designed an experiment where participants observed a video feed of a test subject (in reality, an actor) appearing to receive electrical shocks for responding incorrectly on what was presented as a learning exam. Initially disturbed by the actor's cries of pain, the longer the shocks went on, the more likely the participants were to form negative judgments of the test subject's character.[12]

Many subsequent experiments have replicated this effect, often substituting real-world harms and injustices for the contrived conditions of laboratory experiments. For example, Linda Carli and her colleagues powerfully demonstrated how victim derogation occurs in the context of rape. Their experiments relied on a narrative account of an interaction between a man and a woman, identical except for their endings. One narrative included a neutral ending, whereas the other ended with the man sexually assaulting the woman. The researchers found that participants were more likely to blame and derogate the woman in the sexual assault scenario, compared with the neutral one.[13] A similar victim derogation effect has been established for domestic abuse survivors, those with intellectual disabilities, the global poor, AIDS patients, and even those suffering from indigestion.

With a basic understanding of belief in a just world bias, one can better understand the limitations of privilege politics, which asks us, as one anthologist puts it, to become "conscious that there simply *are* no level playing fields anywhere – and that every single arena, whether class or race or gender or sexuality or religion or anything else, is not just a source of identity but also a site of social inequality that is arbitrary and unfair."[14] If Lerner and other

BJW researchers are correct, becoming conscious of such a reality will be a traumatic affair, one that throws its possessor into a troubling uncertainty about her world, undermines confidence in the effectiveness of her agency, and makes her more rather than less likely to derogate and blame those who are disadvantaged by oppressive systems. Perhaps there is some pedagogical value in creating this kind of discomfort, especially for philosophers like me, who often see their task as one of separating students from their comfortable reliance on questionable truths. But if white students and citizens are really as fundamentally invested in whiteness as many theorists of white privilege suppose (and I suspect that they are), it should not be surprising that they resist the claims of white privilege in the ways that they do, and it may be worthwhile to think about alternative methods that make them more open to such jarring realizations. I will develop such an alternative in the following chapters. But first, let us return to the "psychological wage" of whiteness. With the benefit of nearly a century of social psychology, perhaps we can better understand the psychological bargain that it entails.

* * *

For many political analyses, from Thomas Frank's *What's the Matter with Kansas?* to the cottage industry of post-Trump-election think pieces, the voting behavior and general ideological orientation of working-class white Americans represent a kind of puzzle. Why, these analysts wonder, would working-class whites align themselves with political movements that run counter to their economic interests? Why would they support (to give just one example) a billionaire real estate developer whose most significant legislative accomplishment was a tax cut for the wealthiest Americans and corporations? The Republican Party's strategy of redirecting political discourse away from economics and toward so-called "culture wars" is part of the story here. But to truly understand this phenomenon, one must return to the "wages of whiteness" and consider the appeal and effectiveness of such a strategy.

Here, we can learn from the careful philosophical and psychological analyses of German critical theorist Axel Honneth, whose book *The Struggle for Recognition* demonstrates the centrality of intersubjective relations of recognition to human development and society. Also drawing from empirical psychology, Honneth argues that human development entails three distinct recognitional needs: the need for love, provided initially and largely within familial and intimate relationships; the need for rights, provided within a political system premised on formal legal equality; and the need for social recognition, provided within a culture that acknowledges the unique value of each person and social group. The meeting of these recognitional needs, Honneth argues, is essential to the development of self-confidence, self-respect, and self-esteem in individuals.[15]

One socio-political implication of this view, according to Honneth, is that we misunderstand social movements if we see them as arising primarily out of the deprivation of economic needs. It is not poverty as such nor economic deprivation as such that motivates social movements to demand change, but rather the affront to one's dignity entailed by such deprivation: the sense that one (or one's group) is being disrespected by society.

One can find this sort of demand for recognition underlying social movements that are often perceived to be primarily legal or economic in nature. The American civil rights movement, for example, is often presented simplistically, as a struggle for legal equality and against segregation. However, these legal aims were almost always framed within a context of dignity and respect. Consider Martin Luther King's own reflections on the movement:

> A considerable part of the Negro's efforts of the past decades has been devoted, particularly in the South, to attaining a sense of dignity. For us, enduring the sacrifices of beatings, jailings and even death was acceptable merely to have access to public accommodations. To sit at a lunch counter or occupy the front seat of a bus had no effect on our material standard of living, but in removing a caste stigma it revolutionized our psychology and elevated the spiritual content of our being. Instinctively we struck out for dignity first because personal degradation as an inferior human being was even more keenly felt than material privation.[16]

This emphasis on dignity not only motivated the "public accommodations" sought in the early stages of the movement but continued into its later stages, when it turned more explicitly to issues of poverty and "material deprivation." "The dignity of the individual will flourish," King says, "when the decisions concerning his life are in his own hands, when he has the assurance that his income is stable and certain, and when he knows that he has the means to seek self-improvement."[17]

Similar motives can be seen in revolutionary struggles against colonial occupation. Franz Fanon, perhaps the most influential theorist of such struggles, linked material need to the desire for dignity. "For a colonized people," he observed, "the most essential value, because the most concrete, is first and foremost the land: the land which will bring them bread, and above all dignity"[18] Famously, and contrary to the non-violent methods of King and the U.S. civil rights movement, Fanon argued for the necessity of violence in decolonization, describing it as a "cleansing force" which "frees the native from his inferiority complex...and restores his self-respect."[19] One need not agree with Fanon's views on violence to appreciate his point about dignity and self-respect: that what is most objectionable about colonial subjugation is not the material deprivation of the colonized but rather the disrespect and degradation that colonization entails. In this respect, and despite their other differences, King's and Fanon's views are actually quite similar.

It may seem profane to turn from these storied liberation movements to white grievance politics. However, the same human need for social recognition helps to explain the initial appeal of the "wage" of whiteness as a form of social recognition. If social recognition matters even more than material well-being, then it should not be surprising that working-class whites largely accepted the offer of social superiority in lieu of the economic advances they might have made by acting in solidarity with Black and other workers of color. Further, as society has gradually become more conscious and critical of the white supremacist assumptions undergirding the wages of whiteness, and as the racial deference that whites could once rely on gradually erodes, it should also not surprise us that the most economically precarious whites would lash out in protest at the deflation of the "psychological wage" that once compensated for their precarity.

Again, I do not mean to strike a sympathetic tone regarding the erosion of publicly acknowledged white supremacy, and I certainly don't mean to suggest that such a "wage" be restored. But understanding how and why many white Americans have turned to a form of identity politics, increasingly thinking of themselves as a disfavored minority group, is critical to developing a clear-eyed view of the current state of racial politics, which in turn is critical to developing an effective anti-racist politics.

Consider in this context the striking finding of a ten-year-old survey performed by the Public Religion Research Institute, entitled *Beyond Guns and God: Understanding the Complexities of the White Working Class in America*. The survey found, among other things, that 60% of white working-class Americans agreed with the claim that "discrimination against whites has become as big a problem as discrimination against blacks and other minorities." For those who are familiar with the statistics on racial inequality (nearly all of which favor whites), the racial disproportionalities of the criminal justice system, or other examples of contemporary racial injustice, this claim surely seems absurd. It is tempting to write it off as a simple matter of sociological ignorance. Unfortunately, the survey did not attempt to understand *why* its respondents held this belief, nor what sort of "discrimination" they had in mind. But with Honneth's insight at hand, it seems plausible to think that this belief has less to do with legal discrimination, or even any measurable kind of inequality, and more to do with a perception that the cultural winds have shifted such that white Americans (especially those without the benefits of a college education) no longer enjoy the elevated social status that they once did.

More recent work by the political scientist Ashley Jardina supports this conclusion. Jardina develops a theory of "dominant group identity" focused on explaining how and why racial identity and consciousness become salient to white Americans. She demonstrates that when white cultural dominance goes unchallenged, whites' racial consciousness tends to be low. That is, they are able to see race primarily as a characteristic of racialized others and not as a central feature of their own identity or social status. White racial consciousness increases, however, when "the conditions that facilitate invisibility are disturbed; that is, when the group believes that its status is sincerely challenged."[20] Jardina musters a great deal of empirical evidence to support this theory, noting, for example, reliable correlations between white racial consciousness and views that whites have lost ground politically, economically, and culturally. She finds, for example, that roughly a third of whites who rank highly on a scale of "white identification" agree with the claim that "American society owes whites a better chance in life than they currently have."

Both Jardina's work and the *Beyond Guns and God* survey try to capture a broad range of views held by white Americans, but they take special interest in how these views translate into political opinions. For the older survey, this meant documenting the extent of white working-class support for the Tea Party movement and for presidential candidates Mitt Romney and Barack Obama. For Jardina's more recent work, it meant revealing the correlations between white racial consciousness, perceptions of marginalization, and support for Donald Trump.

In hindsight, it isn't difficult to see how the views and attitudes revealed in the *Beyond Guns and God* survey would develop into Trumpism. But at the time, few could have imagined that Trump's election would thrust the white working class into the center of intense scrutiny and analysis in the way that it did. The following chapter represents my own attempt to make sense of this development and its implications for anti-racist politics. I foreshadow it here only to note how ill-equipped privilege politics is to understand and address it. Not only does the approach run up against powerful and deep-seated cognitive biases, it also fails to understand that its desired converts see themselves not only as not privileged but as actually disadvantaged relative to Americans of color. Of course, democratic politics often entails persuasion, and the attempt to change fellow citizens' minds should not be dismissed. But the scapegoating function of privilege politics renders its attempts at persuasion insincere and unlikely to be successful. Moreover, as I will argue, the attempt to persuade skeptical whites to embrace cross-racial solidarity and anti-racism is much more likely to be successful if framed in terms of self-interest rather than moral obligation, especially when those seeking to convince are viewed as lacking moral authority.

The consequences of failing to effectively engage with this population couldn't be more dire. In the wake of "deflated" (or, perhaps, class-captured) racial privilege, there are two paths forward. One entails the attempt to restore the wage: to re-establish the initial terms of the bargain by fully restoring white supremacy. We see this path represented by a surge in white nationalism and the increased mainstreaming of racist conspiracy theories such as the Great Replacement theory. Some have suggested that it is entailed by Trump's controversial promise to "Make America Great Again." All of these factors have converged like a gathering storm, posing a grave threat not only to racial justice but to democracy itself.

The alternative path involves getting the white working class (and whites in general) to see that the wage of whiteness was a raw deal at the outset, drawing their attention to that which the wage is supposed to compensate for: true social and economic freedom. Moreover, this must be accomplished in such a way that working-class whites can retain their dignity and social esteem, not debasing themselves on the altar of privilege politics but connecting to rich histories of white anti-racism and rural progressivism. It is not an exaggeration to say that is the *only* real path to a flourishing, multicultural, and multiracial democracy.

Notes

1 Kirsten T. Edwards, "This Bridge Called My Body: Talking Race Through Embodying Difference" in George Yancy and Maria del Guadalupe Davidson, eds. *Exploring Race in Predominantly White Classrooms: Scholars of Color Reflect* (New York: Routledge, 2014): 19.

2 Kathy Glass, "Race-ing the Curriculum: Reflections on a Pedagogy of Social Change" in George Yancy and Maria del Guadalupe Davidson, eds. *Exploring Race* (New York: Routledge, 2014): 55.

3 A. Todd Franklin, "A Letter to My Kinfolk on the One Hundred and Fiftieth Anniversary of the Emancipation" in George Yancy and Maria del Guadalupe Davidson, eds. *Exploring Race* (New York: Routledge, 2014): 95.

4 Todd Franklin, *Exploring Race*, 219.

5 Kevin Lally, *Whiteness and Antiracism: Beyond White Privilege Pedagogy* (New York: Teachers College Press, 2022): 17.

6 Kendall, *Understanding White Privilege*, 63.

7 See H. Tajfel, "Experiments in Intergroup Discrimination," *Scientific American* 223 (1970): 96–102; Jeffrey W. Sherman, Steven J. Stroessner, Frederica R. Conroy, and Omar A. Azam, "Prejudice and Stereotype Maintenance Processes: Attention, Attribution, and Individuation," *Journal of Personality and Social Psychology* 89.4 (2005): 607–622; J. Phelan, B.G. Link, R.E. Moore., and A. Stueve, "The Stigma of Homelessness: The Impact of the Label 'Homeless' on Attitudes Toward Poor Persons," *Social Psychology Quarterly* 60.4 (1997): 323–337.

8 J.G. Miller, "Culture and the Development of Everyday Social Explanation," *Journal of Personality and Social Psychology* 46.5 (1984): 961–978.

9 See John T. Jost, Banaji R. Mahzarin, and Brian A. Nosek, "A Decade of System Justification Theory: Accumulated Evidence of Conscious and Unconscious Bolstering of the Status Quo," *International Society of Political Psychology* 25.6 (2004): 881–919; A. Furnham, "Belief in a Just World: Research Progress over the Past Decade," *Personality and Individual Differences* 34 (2003): 795–817.

10 Melvin J. Lerner. *The Belief in a Just World: A Fundamental Delusion* (New York: Plenum Press, 1980): 9.

11 One can see here how attribution bias is involved in the belief in a just world. See Melvin J. Lerner, and Dale T. Miller, "Just World Research and the Attribution Process: Looking Back and Ahead" *Psychological Bulletin* 85.5 (1978): 1030–1051. See also Melvin J. Lerner, "The Desire for Justice and Reactions to Victims," in J. Macaulay, and L. Berkowitz, eds. *Altruism and Helping Behavior* (New York: Academic Press, 1970).

12 Melvin J. Lerner, and C.H. Simmons, "Observer's Reaction to the 'Innocent Victim': Compassion or Rejection?" *Journal of Personality and Social Psychology*, 4 (1966): 203–210.

13 Ronnie Janoff-Bulman, Christine Timko, and Linda L. Carli, "Cognitive Biases in Blaming the Victim," *Journal of Experimental Social Psychology*, 21.2 (1985): 161–177.

14 Michael S. Kimmel, and Abby L. Ferber, eds. *Privilege: A Reader*. 3rd ed. (Boulder, CO: Westview Press, 2013): xi.

15 Axel Honneth, *The Struggle for Recognition: The Moral Grammar of Social Conflicts*. Trans. Joel Anderson (Cambridge, MIT Press, 1996).

16 Martin Luther King, Jr. *Where Do We Go from Here? Chaos or Community?* (Boston: Beacon Press, 2010): 92.

17 Ibid, 173.

18 Franz Fanon, *The Wretched of the Earth*. Trans. Richard Philcox (New York: Grove Press, 2004): 44.

19 Ibid, 93.

20 Ashley Jardina, *White Identity Politics* (Cambridge: Cambridge University Press, 2019): 36.

3

LOST WAGES

A Fork in the Path of Privilege

In the previous chapter, I claimed that the "psychological wage" of whiteness that Du Bois identified and described has experienced a kind of deflation, particularly for its main target, the white working class. This claim stands in need of further defense. Some may be skeptical of it, given that contemporary American society still centers whites, working-class or not, in myriad ways. U.S. film and television still largely cater to white audiences, and critics heap disproportionate praise on white artists, as the #OscarsSoWhite campaign effectively revealed. As for literary culture, a *New York Times* analysis showed that close to ninety percent of all books published in the U.S. are written by white authors, despite non-Hispanic whites making up just under sixty percent of the population.[1] Despite ongoing attempts to diversify curricula, education at all levels continues to center white, European culture and history, relegating the culture and history of peoples of color to the embattled realm of "ethnic studies" (which some states have gone so far as attempting to ban).

Politically, as a result of the complex Electoral College system, the votes of citizens in less populated, largely white states tend to carry more weight than those of citizens in more populated and racially diverse states. The three states whose electoral votes represent the fewest number of people (and thus possess the greatest relative weight per individual voter) are Wyoming, Vermont, and North Dakota. These states are 92, 94, and 87 percent white, respectively. On the other hand, the states whose individual votes are most diluted (representing the largest number of voters per electoral vote), New York, Florida, and California, are among the most racially diverse states in the nation (with California being one of only a few states in the nation where non-Hispanic whites do not constitute a majority). Moreover, as attorney

DOI: 10.4324/9781003461210-4

and legal scholar Matthew Hoffman has argued, the "winner take all" system that all but two U.S. states use to distribute their electoral votes effectively neutralizes the voting power of state-level minorities, where their views differ from the white majority.[2]

Still, these cultural and electoral advantages haven't always translated into concrete material gains for the white working class. Among a certain demographic of white Americans, specifically those without a four-year degree (an imperfect measure that is often used to identify the "working class"), standard of living and even life expectancy have measurably declined, and social instability increased. These declines can be attributed to the demise of manufacturing, declining (actual monetary) wages, deteriorating health outcomes, and other effects of four decades of neoliberal economic policy. This is the "deflation" that I have in mind and will present in detail in this chapter, along with its substantial socio-political consequences. My aim is to navigate between overly sympathetic and blindly critical analyses of the white working class, to ask, with Lise Nelson and her colleagues "what does it mean...to consider with compassion the vulnerabilities of white working-class people while remaining critical of the broader narratives of aggrieved whiteness that undergird contemporary racial formations and racialized violence?"[3] In the post-Trump era, this can be a rather difficult balance to achieve. As the white working class has been (somewhat misleadingly) identified as the key demographic responsible for Trump's election and ongoing influence, analyses tend to fall into two broad categories. On the one hand, investigations of these "forgotten Americans" present a sympathetic picture of a population marginalized by the decline of manufacturing, despised by liberal elites, and ignored by politicians on both sides of the aisle. On the other, analysts focus on racial resentment as the key driver of the Trump voter, emphasizing the anti-immigrant nationalism at the center of Trump's politics and identifying Trump and Trumpism as the logical outcome of the Republican Party's "Southern strategy" of manipulating whites' racial anxiety to gain the allegiance of formerly democratic states and voters.

Political scientist Matthew MacWilliams provides what would appear to be a third alternative. MacWilliams utilized a common authoritarian personality measure to study Trump supporters and claimed as a result of his study that a predisposition to authoritarianism is the single most statistically significant predictor of support for Trump, more significant than race, geography, income, level of education, or any other commonly cited factor.[4] Such authoritarian views allegedly distinguished Trump supporters not only from Clinton-supporting Democrats but also from traditional Republicans supporting candidates other than Trump.

Each of these analyses contains an element of truth. Many of the geographical locations where Trump found the most support are areas where traditional sources of employment have been rendered obsolete or outsourced, where free trade agreements like the North American Free Trade Agreement (NAFTA) are viewed with suspicion, and where the social effects of economic marginalization, manifested in things like drug addiction, have wreaked havoc. On the other hand, it is impossible to ignore the racial dog whistling, scapegoating, and authoritarian tendencies rife within Trumpism.

However, debates about which of these factors has the greatest explanatory salience can easily miss the ways in which they are intertwined. Authoritarian predispositions are activated by threat, with scapegoating discourses representing targeted groups as both economically and existentially threatening. Central American immigrants not only threaten "our" jobs but also are represented as murderers, rapists, and all-around "bad hombres" (as Trump once put it), responsible for increases in crime and disorder. Their perceived threat to law and order is surpassed only by those from the Arab world, who are equated with terrorism and "radical Islam."[5] Such threats, according to authoritarian ideology, must be rooted out by any means necessary, and so racial profiling and increasingly invasive police practices are tolerated within our borders, and broadly restrictive immigration measures, physical barriers, and other imprecise responses are promoted as a means of fortifying those borders. Further, the allegedly existential importance of these measures renders those opposed to them traitors and conspirators, thus encouraging the stifling of dissent and the demonization of political opponents, both key features of authoritarian regimes. Moreover, economic marginalization provides fertile ground for racial scapegoating, which, in turn, serves to fortify authoritarianism and insulate the mechanisms of economic exploitation from popular resistance.

The concept of white privilege fails to capture the intersecting dynamics of economic marginalization, racial scapegoating, and authoritarian rule, especially once it has been divorced from its origins as a critique of racial capitalism. Under the socio-political conditions I describe in this chapter, the demand to acknowledge white privilege (frequently issued from a position of presumed class superiority) only fuels the flames of racial resentment among the white working class. Given the choice between acknowledging white privilege and embracing white identity politics, many working-class whites will inevitably choose the latter.

I will begin, then, by explaining how the white working class has been marginalized within a globalized form of capitalism that increasingly outsources traditional labor and all but requires extensive (and expensive) education as a path to economic stability. The consequences of these developments are not just economic but social, resulting in the rise of what economists Anne Case and Angus Deaton call "deaths of despair."

I then show how this situation lends itself to racial scapegoating and to the radicalization of working-class whites by nationalist, authoritarian, and other reactionary movements. I also describe a subtler and less appreciated form of racial propaganda: misleading narratives about demographic change that claim that whites are poised to become a minority in the U.S.

Having better understood the consequences of the failing politics of privilege, we will be well equipped to turn to the analysis of a more effective alternative approach, one with the capacity to counteract the powerful forms of racial ideology that are currently courting the white working class.

* * *

The fact that the past twenty years have seen a surge of opioid-related deaths has now become well known. Fueled by deregulation and the boundless greed of pharmaceutical companies like Purdue Pharma, the spike in opioid addiction and death led the U.S Department of Health and Human Services to declare the opioid crisis a public health emergency in 2017. Of course, this was far from the first opioid crisis in the United States. In fact, the first wave of opioid addiction arose among Civil War veterans, leading to the country's first drug-related legislation in 1890 and linking the substance to the country's tumultuous racial history from the beginning.

More recently (in the 1970s to be precise), heroin ravaged urban communities of color, leading swiftly to criminalization and a "tough on crime" approach that gave birth to the modern era of mass incarceration. Accordingly, it is hard to shake the sense that the greater attention to the current crisis and the growing trend of viewing addiction as a public health issue rather than a scourge of criminal deviance are related to the perception that addiction now increasingly impacts white communities. Still, the differences between current and past approaches, and the racism that grounds these differences, should not preclude our appreciation of the devastation wrought by addiction in any community. And it should not discourage us from attempting to understand how substance abuse and addiction relate to social and economic upheaval, a phenomenon that the earliest sociologists called "social anomie."

Indeed, it was initially a question about suicide, the backbone of social anomie studied by early sociologists, that led two Princeton economists to discover a shocking trend among middle-aged white Americans. First noticing a substantial increase in suicide deaths among this demographic, Anne Case and Angus Deaton expanded their investigation to discover that not just suicide rates but mortality rates in general were increasing for these Americans. This was especially shocking since, as Deacon and Case put it,

> the steady decrease in death rates, especially in middle age, has been one of the greatest (and most reliable) achievements of the twentieth century, driving up life expectancy at birth not only in the United States but also in other wealthy countries around the world.[6]

That a historically racially advantaged group would be subject to a reversal of this trend is so remarkable that the authors initially thought they had made some mathematical error.

But there was no mistake. The reversal was a result of increases in three categories of mortality: suicides, drug overdoses, and deaths attributed to alcoholic liver disease. Moreover, while these deaths were numerous enough to affect the rates of the broad category of "middle-aged" whites (age 45–54), the bulk of these deaths were concentrated among those middle-aged whites without a bachelor's degree: working-class whites. Whites with at least a four-year college degree were, collectively, exempt from the trend. Provocatively, Case and Deaton described these mortalities as "deaths of despair."

Their explanation for the increase in these deaths points to a general breakdown of community and social structure. As steady, decent-paying employment opportunities erode, less-educated whites not only earn lower incomes and endure greater unemployment but also become less "marriage-able," less likely to be connected to a faith community, less likely to sustain meaningful relationships, and more likely to suffer from mental illness, physical pain, and addiction. That this sort of suffering doesn't always end in death means that the "deaths of despair" measure, shocking as it is, probably underestimates the level of anomie in these communities. Considering this more diffuse, less easily measured kind of suffering along-side mortality rates produces a picture of, in Case and Deaton's words, "a long-term and slowly unfolding loss of a way of life for the white, less educated, working class."[7]

This is the real, qualitative deflation of the "wage" of whiteness. For a group that was promised social superiority to become marginalized in this way (and in such a way that, owing to the role of educational attainment, lends itself to meritocratic rationalizations) creates a tinderbox of resent-ment, anger, and shame. The fact that it is typically educated elites – the meri-tocratic "winners" in terms of educational mobility – who administer regimes of privilege recognition does little to reduce this suffering or neutralize this volatile situation. From the perspective of the "despairing," the moralizing tone of such a politics must seem especially inappropriate and cruel.

Of course, before becoming excessively absorbed in lamentations for the white working class, we must remember, again, that the situation described by Case and Deacon is strikingly similar to the situation experienced by Black Americans in decades gone by (with the notable absence of the systematic removal of millions of those suffering from addiction via mass incarceration). As our economists put it:

> earlier in the twentieth century, blacks faced a mortality crisis precipitated by the arrival of crack cocaine and HIV. This occurred after a period of large-scale job loss for lower-skilled black workers. Jobs in manufacturing and transportation left the inner city, which led to social upheaval,

detachment from the labor force, and a disintegration of family and community life... When the labor market turned against its least skilled workers, blacks were the first to lose out, in part because of their low skill levels, and in part because of longstanding patterns of discrimination. Decades later, less educated whites, long protected by white privilege, were next in line.[8]

When making historical comparisons, people of color may be tempted to draw Dave Chapelle's conclusion. Reflecting on the opioid crisis in his native Ohio in a 2019 comedy special, Chapelle observes to a (presumed) Black audience, "these white folks look exactly like us during the crack epidemic." Accordingly, he claims to glean some insight into "how the white community must have felt watching the Black community go through the scourge of crack."

Then comes the punchline: "because I don't care either."

While such a response might be understandable, it is equally unwise. It is especially unwise for Black Americans, given that Black overdose deaths are now outpacing white deaths again.[9] Even in spite of histories of divergent and discriminatory responses, the commonalities of addiction and its social ramifications in white communities and communities of color have the potential to ground a powerful solidarity. It's tragic that many whites needed to see addiction up close and in their color spectrum before realizing its harrowing destruction. But the realization nonetheless should not be squandered.

Appreciating the social conditions that have given rise to "deaths of despair" in working-class white communities does not support the view that these white Americans somehow have it worse than communities of color (nor that they are the victims of some kind of "reverse discrimination," as the *Beyond Guns and God* survey put it). It does, however, support the view that the "wage of whiteness" has been substantially devalued since the early twentieth-century heyday of white supremacy. This is not a development to be mourned, but it does reveal divergent paths for white working-class politics: the neofascist path seeks to re-establish the wage, reconstructing a social hierarchy with whites firmly established at the top and disciplining those "unruly" social groups that would seek to challenge it. The anti-racist path, by contrast, seeks to build upon common experiences like those associated with anomie-driven addiction to build cross-racial solidarity and thus grow the political power to challenge the root causes of those injustices: an economic system and a miniscule class of owners intent upon ruthless exploitation of the earth and all of its diverse inhabitants. The next chapter will provide a detailed account of the anti-racist path. Now let me describe the neofascist path and the ideological currents that move it.

* * *

If we recall that the original purpose of the "wage of whiteness" and white skin privilege was to protect economic exploitation by precluding interracial solidarity, it should not surprise us that the neofascist attempt to reinstate the wage also seeks to insulate the mechanisms of economic exploitation from interracial resistance. However, whereas chattel slavery, indentured servitude, and (later) wage labor were the common forms of exploitation in the early United States, the mechanisms of exploitation have become more diffuse and complex in the era of globalization. While Americans of all races continue to be subject to economic exploitation, some of the most brutal and lucrative forms of exploitation have migrated to the developing world, leaving less skilled workers in rich countries as likely to be abandoned as enrolled in exploitative regimes of labor. To protect these lucrative global schemes, dissent targeting global capitalism itself must be neutralized or redirected. The result is that the new era of global capitalism has produced dangerous waves of hyper-nationalism around the world. These movements generally involve a vague disdain for "globalism" and "globalists" but reserve their most vehement contempt for vulnerable social groups: racial, religious, and cultural minorities, migrants, and others. By redirecting populist rage toward these groups, whose very vulnerability is often also an effect of globalization, hyper-nationalist movements insulate the global architecture of exploitation from potentially transformational resistance.

This sort of redirection is an instance of what I have called the *scapegoating function* of racialization, and while globalization has re-energized it, it is hardly a new phenomenon. Indeed, scapegoating appears wherever fascism rears its ugly head, as critical theorists and German exiles Max Horkheimer and Theodor Adorno carefully demonstrated.

In their 1947 work *Dialectic of Enlightenment*, Horkheimer and Adorno aimed to show that German anti-Semitism was cultivated as a means of redirecting discontent arising from economic exploitation. In their words, German anti-Semitism served a specific purpose: to "conceal domination in production." While European Jews were historically excluded from ownership of industry, they had, according to Horkheimer and Adorno, achieved some success integrating the "circulation sphere," including what we would now call the financial sector, as well as securing small business ownership. This social position made Jews an easy scapegoat for the most basic injustice of capitalism, the extraction of profit from the wage laborer. This is allegedly because the workers "find out the true nature of the exchange only when they see what they can buy with [their wages]."[10] Thus, the injustice of capitalist wage labor is projected onto the merchant and the banker, and "the economic injustice of the whole class is attributed to him." This produces what Horkheimer and Adorno call a "socially necessary illusion" (necessary, presumably, for the maintenance of the economic status quo, not in any ultimate sense) that "the circulation sphere is responsible for exploitation." This form of scapegoating is expressed finally in their claim that "in the image of the Jew which the racial nationalists hold up before the world they express their own essence."[11] The exploitation that they attribute to the Jewish people is really a projection of their own exploitative nature, and in unleashing violence against these substitute exploiters, the masses feel a false sense of emancipation while remaining within the established "reality principle" of capitalist exploitation.

Interestingly, Horkheimer and Adorno's theory also describes the way that this form of scapegoating relies on what contemporary race theorists call "racialization" – the transformation of a social group into a racial group. Prior to the early twentieth century, and even in the earlier writings of critical theorists, the "Jewish question" was considered to be primarily a matter of cultural and religious difference. As Marx put it, "the most stubborn form of the opposition between the Jew and the Christian is the *religious* opposition."[12] In contrast to this view, Horkheimer and Adorno point out, German fascism understood Jewishness first and foremost in racial terms, thus distancing itself from a "liberal" view which held that "the Jews, free of national or racial features, form a group through religious belief and tradition and nothing else."[13] The Nazis thus attributed to Jews a shared biological essence, solidified in both law and social practice. For example, the Nuremburg Laws, like the so-called "one drop rule" in the United States, included precise specifications of who was to count as Jewish, in order to eliminate any element of voluntary self-identification. In this way, the group targeted for scapegoating is identified and fixed in a more or less stable form.

Racial scapegoating has played a central role in U.S. race relations as well, especially in the gradual dismantling of the welfare state undertaken by neoliberalism. By falsely portraying Black Americans as the primary and undeserving recipients of welfare programs from cash assistance to affordable housing, neoliberal regimes have shored up white support for their assault on those programs, paving the way for a return to an unencumbered capital accumulation that has produced levels of inequality and profitability not seen since before the New Deal. In one revealing study, political scientist Martin Gilens discovered that for white Americans, their attitudes regarding race (and specifically regarding Black Americans) were the single most significant predictor of their views on social welfare programs.[14] Tellingly, these attitudes, including the view that Blacks are "lazy," are more likely to predict opposition to welfare programs even than self-interest (the likelihood that the respondents might receive or be in imminent need of such support themselves). These results are especially striking given that the majority of U.S. welfare recipients are white.

This connection between white racial attitudes and views about social welfare makes welfare policy, like so many other topics in U.S. politics, rife with racial undertones and thus prone to manipulation through what Ian Haney Lopez calls "dog whistle politics." Such a politics, perfected over decades by the U.S. Republican Party, consists in garnering support through racially coded appeals that are "inaudibly and easily denied in one range, yet stimulating strong reactions in another."[15] While the racial scapegoating of the

Third Reich was explicit and unapologetic, contemporary scapegoating of "illegal" immigrants, criminal "thugs," "welfare queens," and more blankets itself under dog whistles to conceal its racist character and to avail itself of plausible deniability against charges of racism. Still, the function of racial scapegoating remains the same: to insulate broadly harmful forms of exploitation from popular understanding and criticism. As Haney Lopez puts it, such racial appeals "constitute the dark magic by which middle-class voters have been convinced to turn government over to the wildly affluent, notwithstanding the harm this does to themselves."[16]

This "dark magic" – these clever attempts to sustain systems of exploitation through manipulative political rhetoric – is part of what Marxists call "ideology." Ideology, in the Marxist sense, refers not simply to a set of interrelated ideas or theories but to such a set of ideas designed to rationalize and sustain a specific system of economic relations. One need not be a Marxist, though, to appreciate the way in which racial ideology serves this function. Obscuring the fact that the decline of working-class white communities is a direct correlate of the rise of unrestrained global capitalism, scapegoating, dog whistling, and other elements of racial ideology shift the blame to Americans of color, encouraging whites to assume that their privileges have been "transferred" to competing social groups rather than understanding that their standard of living has eroded along with everyone else's. Bell hooks makes this point effectively in her powerful analysis of race–class intersectionality, *Where We Stand: Class Matters*. While acknowledging the racial disproportionality of poverty, hooks nonetheless notes that, given U.S. demographics, the majority of U.S. poor are white. Concealing this fact, she argues, serves an ideological function:

> Better to have poor and working-class white folks believe white supremacy is still giving them a meaningful edge than to broadcast the reality that the poor of any race no longer have an edge in this society, or that downsizing daily drags previously economically sound white households into the ranks of the poor.[17]

Given this pattern of obfuscation, hooks refers to the white poor as the "hidden face" of poverty and notes their near invisibility in American culture. Let us return to the politics of privilege with this fact in mind, to discover the role that it plays in this ideological scheme.

As described in Chapter 1, the politics of privilege engages in its own form of scapegoating, drawing on class divisions rather than racial differences to offer misleading explanations of racial injustice. Its first misstep is simply failing to acknowledge the decline in the prospects of the white working class. By focusing exclusively on racial privilege, it forestalls any recognition of intra-racial class disadvantage and thus misses a crucial opportunity to build solidarity and understanding. Much has been written about the ways that "color blindness" – the insistence that racial equality entails denying and ignoring racial difference – covertly sustains racial inequality. But little has been said about the ways that *class* blindness achieves the same effect vis-à-vis class-based inequality and exploitation. By methodologically denying or bracketing class-based differences, the politics of privilege keeps such hierarchies comfortably unchallenged. Further, as we have seen, this disadvantage is not balanced by any great advancement in racial justice. Despite a rhetoric of "social transformation," privilege politics rarely moves beyond the liberal framework of subjective moral and psychological conversion, which is typically achieved by educated, middle- and upper-class whites, at the expense of working-class whites.[18]

With this in mind, and without being exceedingly conspiratorial, one can see that privilege politics too plays its role in sustaining the status quo of racial injustice, both by alienating a demographic whose support is critical to real change and by offering a pseudo-solution that allows powerful institutions to claim that they are doing their part without fundamentally risking their established place or power.

* * *

Not all forms of racial ideology are as nefarious as the Third Reich's scapegoating of Jews or the criminalization and incarceration of Black Americans. Sometimes, racial ideology works in more subtle and insidious ways, taking the form, for example, of seemingly neutral demographic analysis. Such is the case with the cottage industry of commentaries on the U.S. Census Bureau's regularly misunderstood statistics on racial demographics.

A simple internet search of the combined terms "white" and "minority" produces hundreds if not thousands of articles reporting roughly the same "facts." Owing to increased immigration from non-European countries, the comparatively higher birth rates of these immigrants, and other factors, whites, the chorus goes, will soon become a minority in the United States. The typical time line places the tipping point for this "majority minority" scenario at roughly the middle of the 21st century.

As with much propaganda, there is a kernel of truth to these predictions. The projections point to real demographic changes in the contemporary United States, driven by the elimination of racist immigration policies that gave preference to white European migrants. These racist policies are at least as old as the U.S. itself, with the country's first immigration policy, the Naturalization Act of 1790, limiting citizenship to "free white persons" of "good moral character." And while this act was technically invalidated by the passage of the Fourteenth Amendment, implicit and explicit racial exclusion continued to drive immigration policy for another hundred years. The

Immigration Act of 1924, for example, attempted to manage racial demographics in an ostensibly race-neutral way, via the "national origins" formula, which limited the number of immigrants from any one country to 2% of the number of the existing U.S. citizens of that national background. The national origins formula thus effectively preserved the existing racial demographic of the country, a goal which its authors were not shy about making explicit. It was only with the passage of the Immigration Act of 1965 that the national origins formula was abolished, and the stage was set for a significant shift in the sources of the U.S. immigrant population. Previous to 1965, eight of the top ten countries of origin of U.S. immigrants were in Europe (the exceptions being Canada and Mexico). In 2020, by contrast, no European countries even appeared in the top ten. Mexico represented the largest source of immigration by far with 10.8 million Mexican-born Americans, followed by China and India with around 2.7 million each. The rest of the top ten was (and remains) populated by a combination of other Latin American and Asian nations, including Vietnam, The Philippines, the Dominican Republic, Cuba, El Salvador, Korea, and Guatemala.

So it is certainly true that the geographical sources of U.S. immigration have shifted significantly, away from European countries and toward Latin American and Asian nations. And the common understanding of "white" as meaning something like "of European heritage" would seem to suggest that the claim about white minority follows logically from this shift. But upon closer analysis, the claim proves to be misleading. To see why, one can begin by looking at the U.S. Census Bureau's actual population projections, the source of almost all of the alarmist claims about impending white minority (for those commentaries responsible enough to care about sources).

If you look closely at these projections, you will notice that they do not actually make the claim so frequently attributed to them. In 2016, the population of those who reported only one race, white, was around 248 million, just under 77% of a total population of 323.2 million. This population is projected to increase steadily to 272 million in 2050, not quite keeping pace with the projected increase in the general population to 389 million but remaining a majority at 70% of the population.[19]

So where do the claims of white minority find empirical support? It is only after separating "race" from "ethnicity," particularly "Hispanic" ethnicity, that *non-Hispanic* whites appear to be declining toward minority. Then the 2016 population of non-Hispanic whites (198 million, or 61% of the general population) gradually decreases as a percentage of the general population until it falls under 50% around 2043.

This is much more than a technicality. It represents a serious conceptual confusion on the part of those who have interpreted the data to say that "whites" are destined to become a minority (again, the report itself makes no such claim). It also demonstrates a significant tension between the fact that a majority of Hispanic Americans identify as white and white alone (at least for the purposes of the Census) and the norm of thinking about Hispanic and Latinx persons as "persons of color." The more thoughtful and careful demographic analyses do note these difficulties. One warns that

> These projections assume that definitions of race and ethnic categories will remain fixed and that self-identification does not change over time. In reality, the growing numbers of births to parents of different racial and ethnic groups, as well as changing social norms about racial and ethnic self-identification, are serving to blur the boundaries of racial/ethnic categories. Consequently, the future sizes of race/ethnic groups could be higher or lower than the projection values even if the underlying demographic assumptions about the future prove to be correct.[20]

Further, it is not just "self-identification" that changes over time, but how we think about race itself and about who counts as white. As we saw in Chapter 1, the common conception of whiteness has shifted dramatically over time, with non-protestant, non-Anglophone Europeans often being considered non-white. This explains the Breitbart-esque hand-wringing of one Benjamin Franklin, sounding the 18th-century alarm about the "Palatine Boors" (Germans), who had begun to "swarm into our Settlements, and by herding together establish their Language and Manners to the Exclusion of ours." Franklin asks, polemically, "why should Pennsylvania, founded by the English, become a Colony of Aliens, who will shortly be so numerous as to Germanize us instead of our Anglifying them, and will never adopt our Language or Customs, any more than they can acquire our Complexion."[21]

Indeed, the threat to "whiteness" posed by "swarthy" European groups was the primary motivator for the "national origins" formula discussed above. The two decades preceding its passage saw Theodore Roosevelt encouraging "white" women to procreate at a rate that would prevent "race suicide" in the face of increasing immigration from Southern and Eastern Europe.[22]

So the current panic over "non-white" immigration is nothing new, and sadly, demographic trends alone are at least as likely to create a new class of "white" Americans as they are to dissolve centuries of white supremacy. This is especially likely considering that Latin America has its own history of white supremacy, grounded in anti-indigenous prejudice and a less binary (though still quite rigid) racial hierarchy.

* * *

The inaccuracy of these projections has not decreased their frequency or social currency. The numbers lend a presumed legitimacy to conclusions like that of the *LA Times*, which, the morning after Barack Obama had won re-election over white Republican challenger Mitt Romney, declared the election "the end of the world as straight white males know it." They provide a cover of data-driven objectivity to political analysts who observe that there aren't enough "middle-aged white guys" left for this or that candidate to pander to. But they also serve a more insidious ideological function.

Accurate or not, these predictions represent a clarion call to white Americans to protect their power, status, and resources from non-white encroachment. In past ages, this sort of appeal could be made explicitly. The difference in the post–civil rights era is that public appeals to white supremacy are no longer considered morally legitimate in the way that they once were. Either attempts to secure white domination must therefore be encoded in some ostensibly race-neutral way (via dog whistling and race-implicit scapegoating) or else whiteness itself must be re-imagined as a threatened minority rather than a dominant majority. Predictions of white minority play a key ideological role in the latter objective. Whether or not they are likely to be accurate, they have been incredibly successful in shaping white worldviews.

Going back at least a decade, studies have shown that white Americans *already* believe themselves to have crossed the dreaded precipice of minorityhood. One survey by sociologist Charles Gallagher saw whites estimating their proportion of the population at just under 50% at a time when the actual proportion was just over 75%.[23] Strikingly, these same whites tended to significantly overestimate the proportion of racial minorities, especially when they had little actual contact with them. Many respondents explicitly mentioned reports about whites becoming a minority as a factor in their misperceptions. Moreover, white estimates of relative population size seem to be closely linked to perceptions about relative power and status.

We have already encountered the survey that saw 53% of working-class white Americans agreeing that "discrimination against whites has become as big a problem as discrimination against blacks and other minorities." This finding is closely related to perceptions about declining and ascendant social groups. In Gallagher's study, when he confronted his survey respondents with accurate population figures and challenged them to explain the discrepancy with their own estimations, they mentioned not only reports of impending white minority but also their perception that minorities, Blacks especially, were more vocal and demanding politically and more willing to engage in identity politics as a means of securing power and resources. The following response from "Pam," a middle-aged white woman from an almost entirely white county in rural Georgia, is representative:

> I think that blacks are more vocal about what they want, wanting their rights ... It's just like in this county when blacks wanted the right to vote ... they didn't hesitate to get out, march up and down the street calling

attention to themselves. And we, the white people, will sit around and gripe about it, but we won't get up and take to the streets and march ... We are not as obvious out there ... We tend to, I think, sit back and maybe gripe about things, and the blacks will get up, march around and be vocal and, you know, demand what they want.[24]

This kind of response reveals that not only do perceptions of group size lead to anxiety about relative power but also perceptions of relative power can influence perceptions of group size. It stands to reason that whites who perceive themselves as a numerical minority, and who perceive themselves as lacking power as a result, might follow the example of other minority groups that they perceive to have advocated successfully for their own advancement.

In this way, the mythology of white minority provides a framework for actively furthering white supremacy even more directly than dog whistling or racial scapegoating. Representing whites as a minority paves the way for a symmetrical view of white and non-white identity politics. Whereas there is a clear (though often ignored) moral asymmetry between the claims of a dominant majority and those of a historically oppressed minority – for example, between "white pride" and "Black pride" – the reconstitution of whites as a minority aims to place the two on level moral ground. If whites are a minority, and if this entails, as many whites suppose, loss of political and cultural dominance, then attempts to advance (presumed) white interests, promote white "culture," and secure white power appear no longer as racist but rather as demands for recognition within a multicultural political framework, no different from those of other minority groups. This is the essence of the "white identity politics" that we encountered in the previous chapter, and the myth of white minority aids and abets it by, as Gallagher puts it, "maintaining and simultaneously masking racial dominance." Alongside dog whistling and scapegoating, it represents a critical piece of contemporary racial ideology.

At its most extreme, the mythology of white minority lends itself to white supremacist violence. French fascist Renaud Camus' *The Great Replacement* has provided the reactionary right with a façade of intellectual sophistication, arguing that the resettlement of non-Christian migrants in Europe amounts to a global conspiracy to "replace" white Christian Europeans. As his ideas have gained global influence among far-right nationalists, many followers have adopted the dangerous rhetoric of "white genocide" to capture the alleged phenomenon. Predictably, the view has motivated multiple acts of racial terrorism. In Charleston, South Carolina, a twenty-one-year-old white man convinced that Black Americans were "taking over the country" entered a historic African-American church and murdered nine worshipers. His online manifesto notes his transformative "realization" that "the same things were happening in England and France, and in all the other Western European countries." In Buffalo, New York, an eighteen-year-old white man entered a supermarket in a Black neighborhood and executed ten Black shoppers. His manifesto cites the Great Replacement theory explicitly and notes his admiration for the Charleston shooter as well as other white terrorists, including the perpetrator of a mass shooting in a Christchurch, New Zealand mosque, who killed 51 worshipers. In a Walmart in El Paso, Texas, another twenty-one-year-old white male targeted Hispanic Americans, killing 23 shoppers in what has been described as the deadliest attack on that group in modern American history. He too cites the Great Replacement theory explicitly as well as the influence of the Christchurch mosque shooting.

In the United States, where such mass shootings are tragically common, responses generally focus on lax gun control laws or (less frequently) inadequate mental health care. Rarely do they wrestle with the racist backbone of this growing form of mass violence, even when a 2020 report from the U.S. Department of Homeland Security named white supremacist terrorism the deadliest domestic terrorism threat facing the country.[25]

It would go too far to say that the politics of privilege is directly responsible for this latest chapter of U.S. racial terrorism. However, as we have seen, its failure to reach a substantial number of working-class white Americans – indeed, its attempt to make of them a scapegoat for systemic racial oppression – means that this demographic will continue to be susceptible to radicalization by a highly organized and motivated movement of neo-fascists. The racial terrorism and violence that they carry out then become something of a self-fulfilling prophecy, confirming liberal suspicions that these psychologically unstable, bigoted, privilege-denying whites are indeed the root of the country's race problem.

Camille Gear Rich's analysis of "marginal whiteness" further demonstrates the culpability of privilege politics in the radicalization of working-class whites. "When scholars talk about white privilege in the abstract," she argues, "without discussing the host of competing identity variables that complicate white privilege, they risk increasing the salience of whiteness for less race-identified whites."[26] Those who might be inclined to "betray" a whiteness that bestows uneven or unreliable advantage are instead chastised for denying their privilege. Conversely, by acknowledging the differential, class-structured distribution of racial privilege, and by acknowledging that white supremacy can and does harm working-class whites as well as people of color, Rich argues that we can create space for strengthening interracial resistance to racial injustice and class-based resistance to economic injustice alike.

It is clear that an alternative to privilege-based approaches is necessary. It is possible to address the long-neglected needs of communities of color without scapegoating working-class white communities with their own genuine problems. Indeed, upon closer analysis, it becomes apparent that many of these problems look similar across racial lines and are traceable to common causes. Political analyses that draw attention to these causes have the potential to create cross-racial solidarity while allowing all Americans to retain a sense of dignity, belonging, and self-worth. The wages of whiteness cannot and should not be reinstated. But whites can return to the bargaining table, strengthened by the support of their fellow Americans, empowered to address the deep-rooted forms of exploitation from which the "psychological wage" strategy aims to distract. I call such an alternative an "interest convergence" approach. Let me now, finally, describe it in more detail.

Notes

1　Richard Jean So, and Gus Wezerek, "Just How White Is the Book Industry?" *New York Times*. December 11, 2020.
2　Matthew M. Hoffman, "The Illegitimate President: Minority Vote Dilution and the Electoral College," *The Yale Law Journal* 105.4 (January, 1996): 935–1021.
3　Lise Nelson, Barbara E. Smith, and Jamie Winders, "Between Aggrieved Whiteness and Class Precarity: A Feminist Politics of Interpretation," *Gender, Place, and Culture: A Journal of Feminist Geography* 29.7 (2022): 2.
4　Matthew C. MacWilliams, *The Rise of Trump: America's Authoritarian Spring*. (Amherst: Amherst University Press, 2016).
5　See Falguni Sheth, *Toward a Political Philosophy of Race* (Albany: SUNY Press, 2009); George Fourlas, "Being a Target: On the Racialization of Middle Eastern Americans," *Critical Philosophy of Race* 3.1 (2015): 101–123.
6　Anne Case, and Angus Deaton, *Deaths of Despair and the Future of Capitalism* (Princeton: Princeton University Press, 2021): 2.
7　Ibid, 146.
8　Ibid, 62.
9　Brian Mann, "Black Americans are Now Dying from Drug Overdoses at a Higher Rate than Whites," *NPR News*. March 2, 2022.
10　Max Horkheimer, and Theodor Adorno, *The Dialectic of Enlightenment: Philosophical Fragments*. Trans. Edmund Jephcott (Stanford: Stanford University Press, 2007): 142.
11　Ibid, 137.
12　Karl Marx, "On the Jewish Question," in Robert Tucker, ed. *The Marx-Engels Reader* (New York: Norton & Company, 1978): 26–46, 28. Original Emphasis.
13　Horkheimer and Adorno, *The Dialectic of Enlightenment*, 137.
14　Martin Gilens, "'Race Coding' and White Opposition to Welfare," *The American Political Science Review* 90.3 (1996): 593–604.
15　Ian Haney Lopez, *White By Law: The Legal Construction of Race* (New York: NYU Press, 2006): 3.
16　Ibid.
17　bell hooks, *Where We Stand: Class Matters* (London: Routledge, 2000): 117.
18　See Lisa R. Pruitt, "Who's Afraid of White Class Migrants? On Denial, Discrediting, and Disdain (and Toward a Richer Conception of Diversity), *Columbia Journal of Gender and Law* 31 (2015) for a compelling account of how working-class and poor whites are marginalized in academic settings and in academic understandings of diversity.
19　See *Projected Race and Hispanic Origin: Main Projection Series for the Unites States, 2017–2060*. U.S. Census Bureau, Population Division. Washington, D.C. 2018.

20 Jeffery Passel, and D'Vera Cohn, "U.S. Population Projections: 2005–2050," *Washington D.C. Pew Hispanic Center*. February 11, 2008: 14. To their point, in 2023, the Biden administration proposed significant changes to the way that the 2030 Census will utilize racial and ethnic categories. If the proposed changes are enacted, the previously separate categories of "race" and "ethnicity" will be collapsed into one category, asking respondents about their "race or ethnicity," with "Hispanic or Latino" being one of the possible responses. The effects of such changes, including on the population of "white" Americans, could be dramatic, especially if they include a dramatic reduction of "Hispanic whites," as seems likely.

21 Benjamin Franklin, "Observations Concerning the Increase of Mankind and the Peopling of Countries," in *The Autobiography and Other Writings* (New York: Oxford University Press, 2008): 251–260, 259.

22 See Theodore Roosevelt, "On American Motherhood." Speech given before the National Congress of Mothers. March 13, 1905. See also Thomas Dyer. *Theodore Roosevelt and the Idea of Race* (Baton Rouge: Louisiana State University Press, 1992); and Nell Irvin Painter's chapter on "Roosevelt, Ross, and Race Suicide," in her book, *The History of White People* (New York: WW Norton, 2010): 245–256.

23 Charles A. Gallagher. "Miscounting Race: Explaining Misperceptions in Racial Group Size," *Sociological Perspectives* 46.3 (2003): 381–396.

24 Ibid, 387–388.

25 See Department of Homeland Security, *Homeland Threat Assessment*. October, 2020.

26 Camille Gear Rich, "Marginal Whiteness," *California Law Review* 98.5 (October 2010): 1565.

4

INTEREST CONVERGENCE

Forging a Path to Racial and Economic Justice

In the weeks leading up to the 2016 U.S. presidential election, *Saturday Night Live* ran a version of its recurring skit *Black Jeopardy*, with host Tom Hanks playing "Doug," a MAGA hat–wearing, vaguely Southern (though easily Midwestern) Trump supporter, alongside Black cast members Kenan Thompson, Leslie Jones, and Sasheer Zamata. A common comedic strategy, the skit builds and then dissolves tension (in this case, racial tension) in its constructed scenario.

In the beginning, host Darnell Hayes (Thompson) questions Doug's credentials, asking skeptically "you sure you ready to play *Black* Jeopardy"? But his skepticism soon subsides as he realizes Doug is quite adept. His correct responses span the realms of conspiracy (of a new feature of iPhones requiring a thumbprint to unlock the device, Doug correctly responds "What is, 'that's how they get you'." To the answer "they out here saying every vote counts," Doug offers the correct corresponding question "what is, 'come on, they already decided who wins even before it happens'"), economic communalism (another correct response invokes "that dude in my neighborhood who will fix anything for forty dollars"), and cultural and religious commonality (one punch line has Doug praising a Tyler Perry box set he bought at Walmart: "If I can laugh and pray in 90 minutes, that is money well spent"). In the end, though, the racial tension is reintroduced, as the host notes the *Final Jeopardy* category: *Lives that Matter*.

Good comedy often reveals uncomfortable truths, and with over 75 million views, this sketch seems to have hit upon something important about Black–white relations in the Trump era (and in American history more generally). It may seem trite, but it is nonetheless accurate: in spite of a history of tension and violence, and the white supremacist mythology entailed by the

DOI: 10.4324/9781003461210-5

"psychological wage" of whiteness, Black, and poor and working-class white Americans have much more in common than they (especially whites) might like to believe.

I noticed these commonalities long before 2016, as my own family tree includes a branch of working-class white transplants, having migrated, like many Black families, from the rural South and Appalachia to industrial northern cities. In my family's case, they were drawn to the automobile factories of mid-twentieth-century Detroit, along a migration path some scholars refer to as the "Hillbilly Highway." From a young age, I was puzzled by some of these relatives' anti-Black racism, grounded in stereotypes that "hillbillies" and poor whites were themselves often subject to: poor hygiene, loud and brash demeanors, tacky home decor, sexual deviance, and more. And beyond stereotypes, the realities of their lives often seemed quite similar too, from their Southern Baptist faith to their manner of speaking and notions of comfort food.

Of course, this is due largely to the fact that African-Americans, Southern whites, and (perhaps to a lesser degree) white Appalachians often share an overlapping culture, which at times has placed them outside of the norms and mobility pathways of the northern cities where many ended up. This is not to say that things were *equally* hard for Black and white migrants. Nor is to assume that the Southern social norms that put Blacks and whites in closer contact than was acceptable in the North were not compatible with deeply oppressive social hierarchies. It is only to note that the same similarities that plantation elites in the antebellum South worried would give rise to interracial solidarity persist into the present and make the possibility of such solidarity an enduring alternative to the divisive path of white supremacy.

These similarities include not just shared cultural experiences but, as we have seen, overlapping economic interests. From slavery to the present, the actions and policies of those who claim to represent white interests often harm working-class whites as well (if not always as much) as their fellow Americans of color. This is the core thesis of political analyst Heather McGhee's recent book *The Sum of Us: What Racism Costs Everyone and How We Can Prosper Together*. McGhee begins with the story of a boom in the construction of public swimming pools in the first part of the 20th century. Competing with each other to provide the most lavish, resort-like facilities for their residents, over 2,000 U.S. communities had constructed public pools by the onset of World War II. McGhee characterizes this boom, funded in part by the Depression-era Works Progress Administration, as a forgotten "Americanizing project." Like public schools, these facilities were designed as "social melting pots," intended to "overcome ethnic divisions and cohere a common identity."[1] Yet such a goal was severely tested by the desegregation mandates of the civil rights era, and many white communities resisted the prospect of sharing their pools with Black swimmers. The predictable result was the closure of the vast majority of these facilities, drained, filled, abandoned, and left to be reclaimed by nature.

The lesson in this historical allegory resonates clearly into the 21st century. By acquiescing to racism, white Americans lost access to a valuable resource right along with those they sought to exclude. McGhee applies this lesson to a wide variety of more consequential contexts: public education, housing, labor organizing, environmental justice, and, ultimately, the functionality of democracy itself. We have seen at least one such example already: by portraying hard-won social benefits as the undeserved spoils of Black and other Americans of color, neoliberal policy makers won white support for dismantling a social safety net that protected them more than anyone. A similar fate has befallen education. As more students of color have gained access to public universities, state funding of those institutions has decreased, leaving students of all races with massive, life-altering debt. In other cases, white indifference to injustices experienced by people of color allows such injustice to expand and ensnare white communities. For example, the predatory lending practices that crashed the global economy in 2008, decimating the wealth of middle-class whites who were previously sheltered by racially discriminatory housing policies, were tested and honed in communities of color. Ongoing attacks on Black voting rights disenfranchise poor and working-class whites. And perhaps most significantly, accelerating climate change risks the very life of the species but is often ignored because its harms are perceived to concentrate in communities of color.

Examples like these, some of which I discuss in the following chapter, highlight what McGhee calls the "solidarity dividend," the concrete benefits that whites stand to gain by standing with and for communities of color (or lose out on when they fail to do so). If there is any legitimate compensation to be had for the devalued wage of whiteness, it must be found in something like a solidarity dividend. The search for such common benefits is at the heart of what I call an "interest convergence" approach to racial and economic justice, an alternative to the moralizing approach of privilege politics, which, as we have seen, expects of whites something which (it assumes) is actually *against* their interest and which it is unlikely that those not already convinced of their moral superiority are likely to adopt.

* * *

While the politics of privilege has been thoroughly captured by ameliorative liberalism, the theory of interest convergence seeks inspiration from liberalism's critics, both those who originally articulated the self-defeating nature of the "wage of whiteness" and "white skin privilege" and those who were already beginning to recognize the failures of liberal anti-racism at the onset of neoliberalism in the 1980s. The latter includes the important and widely misunderstood work of critical race theory, a movement of legal scholars who studied the ways that racial oppression has entrenched itself in social and legal systems despite the civil rights movement's eradication of most *de jure* forms of racial discrimination.

Derrick Bell, a civil rights lawyer, legal scholar, and one of the movement's founders, famously argued that racial progress tends to occur only when it coincides with the interests of whites. Bell's analysis of the civil rights movement – and especially the movement toward desegregation grounded in the *Brown v. Board of Education* decision – held that these developments were not the result of an intrinsic trajectory toward racial justice, nor even of an acknowledgement on the part of the legal system of the injustice of its own history, but rather of a historical moment in which the domestic policy of the United States toward Black Americans was undermining the legitimacy of its Cold War pretensions to be a global beacon of freedom and liberation. Insofar as this image was perceived to be crucial to the U.S. national interest, a measure of equality was granted to Black Americans that had until then been withheld, as it would not have benefitted white elites to grant it. Moreover, Bell points out that state-sponsored segregation was viewed by some powerful whites as a barrier to Southern industrialization. In Bell's view, then, it was this convergence of Black and white interests that explains the much-celebrated advances of the civil rights era.[2]

Bell dubbed this an "interest convergence" view, and along with his "racial realism," which surmised that racism was a permanent feature of American society, it is often interpreted as a pessimistic challenge to the optimism of liberal civil rights discourses. But the view is not merely a negative critique, nor is it without its own implications for pursuing racial justice. Once one abandons the politically naïve view that racial justice comes about primarily through the moral transformation of previously immoral individuals or institutions, one can refocus on identifying, articulating, and expanding areas of overlapping interest among whites and people of color.

The idea that movements for justice and social change need to appeal to the self-interest of their constituents and desired converts is an established pillar of community-organizing wisdom. Unfortunately, many allegedly progressive movements and initiatives within academia ignore this basic piece of organizing knowledge. Perhaps this is due to the population they typically engage: younger students whose interests are not yet fixed, whom they may presume they can mold into compliance with (their) established moral standards. At any rate, academic anti-racism can no longer proceed in this way, ignoring the perceived or actual interests of large swaths of the population or considering them only as a foil by which to confirm their own moral righteousness.

Combatting the radicalization of the white working class means demonstrating the myriad ways that systemic racism harms, not serves them. While white Americans certainly enjoy various advantages grounded in the continuing existence of racism and white supremacy, it is also true that for the majority of them, the security of their jobs, the health of their bodies and minds, the responsiveness of their government, the education of their children, and many other things besides are hampered by the existence of racial injustice. This provides them with self-interested reasons to resist racism and seek out interracial solidarity.

This does not mean that all anti-racist efforts must center their work on the interests of white Americans, nor even that all racial justice work needs to be interracial. Communities of color need not ignore their own needs in favor of building bridges with white communities. Rather, an effective interest convergence approach is consistent with communities of color articulating their own interests internally instead of being forced to accede to the dominant interests of whites. That is, it is consistent with what is often understood as "identity politics," the pursuit of political goals and initiatives seeking justice primarily for one's own identity group.

Acknowledging the validity of this sort of approach, however, does not preclude the recognition that, while identity politics may achieve some important proximate goals (provided it is not "captured" by elites in the way that Taiwo describes), realizing ultimate racial and economic justice in multiracial class societies necessarily entails cooperation and negotiation across identity groups. Despite common misunderstanding, this insight is not inconsistent with identity politics as conceived by its most thoughtful original practitioners. Black Nationalists like Stokely Carmichael, for example, reminded his followers that "the advocates of Black Power do *not* eschew coalitions; rather we want to establish the grounds on which we feel political coalitions can be viable."[3] The Black feminist *Combahee River Collective*, often cited as the conceptual originators of contemporary identity politics, described themselves as "doing political work within our own group and in coalition with other progressive organizations and movements" and confirmed that they were "actively committed to struggling against racial, sexual, heterosexual, and class oppression, and see as our particular task the development of integrated analysis and practice based upon the fact that the major systems of oppression are interlocking."[4] This intersectional emphasis belies the common trope that identity politics is single-mindedly focused on the concerns of an internally homogenous group and opposed to approaches that aim to identify interests across identity groups.

The intersecting interests of the white working class and Americans of color require more attention than they have received in recent years. Yet, to state the obvious, these are not the only interests relevant to an interest convergence approach in racially, culturally, and otherwise diverse societies. Unfortunately, the interest convergence approach has historically been associated with class-reductionist views that dismiss racism as a distraction from an allegedly more primary class-based social conflict. Yet there is no principled reason why an interest convergence approach needs to prioritize the interests of some groups over others or of some forms of social conflict over others. The fact that this has usually been the case is the result of a historical contingency: that the purveyors of class-based interest convergence in the United States have typically been white, dismissive of the agency and experience of people of color, and more interested in gaining support for their own cause than in forging genuinely collaborative coalitions. An interest convergence approach to racial and economic justice must avoid repeating these costly mistakes.

In the end, the most compelling defense of an interest convergence alternative to the politics of privilege consists in a detailed presentation of specific interests that cut across racial lines. I will provide such a defense in the following chapter. But first, let me briefly outline the ways that an interest convergence approach fares better in terms of the psychological barriers and biases that undermine the effectiveness of privilege-based approaches.

* * *

Recall from Chapter 2 that privilege politics is hampered by attribution biases, which encourage people to see their advantages as earned and to see the disadvantages of others as deserved. These biases are closely related to system justification biases like Belief in a Just World (BJW) bias, which encourage us to interpret the status quo as just and to blame and stigmatize victims of injustice. These biases shape individual attitudes, but they also generalize to the level of groups, resulting in worldviews that rationalize both privilege and disadvantage in ways that can undermine anti-racist aims (especially when framed in terms of white privilege). But interestingly, while race is an undeniably powerful marker of difference, it is not an insurmountable one. Certain situations manifest perceived commonalities that can, at least temporarily, trump racial differences and therefore reorganize the parameters of biased attribution.

Remember Melvin Lerner's electric shock experiment, the one that established the "victim derogation" effect? Interestingly, when the experiment was preceded by a lottery in which either the observer or the actor was supposedly chosen at random to receive the shocks, the observer was far less likely to derogate the victim. To the contrary, this and other experimental conditions actually resulted in victim *enhancement*. A similar experiment assigned participants the role of either worker or supervisor and then had them observe and evaluate a situation in which a supervisor accidentally ruins the work of a worker. Those who were categorized as supervisors tended to derogate the worker and explained the supervisor's actions in relation to external factors like poor equipment. Those who were categorized as workers, however, tended not to see the worker in a negative light, instead blaming the supervisor for the outcome, referencing internal characteristics like poor management ability.[5] This demonstrates that attribution and BJW bias can be alleviated when one perceives a commonality between oneself and the victims of injustice or circumstance or when one can easily see oneself in the victim's place. By identifying grounds for cross-racial solidarity, an interest convergence approach to anti-racism can take advantage of this effect, mitigating victim derogation by emphasizing concrete commonalities and shared interests.

The increasing (though by no means universal) recognition of the contingent, non-biological character of racial identity also bodes well for an interest convergence approach. Social psychologists have shown that the less permeable group boundaries are perceived to be, the more likely group members are to attempt to elevate their social status by denigrating out-groups or valorizing their own group. On the other hand, when group boundaries are perceived to be less fixed, individuals are more likely to dissociate from group memberships and pursue alternative strategies for social advancement.[6] In this context, cross-racial solidarity grounded in shared economic interest may become an appealing strategy.

Here, arguments about the changing racial demographics of the United States actually have greater bearing. As I argued in Chapter 3, predictions about whites becoming a minority are misleading at best, given their failure to appreciate that understandings of whiteness, and racial categories generally, shift over time. But as sociologist Richard Alba argues, the changing demographics of the U.S. is not just a macro-level phenomenon. It has also transformed households, with one in six American families being grounded in mixed-race relationships.[7] Relatedly, an increasing number of Americans identify with more than one race, dealing a further blow to the idea of race as a monolithic identity and of racial "minorities" as monolithically "other." Finally, longitudinal social science research has revealed that it is not uncommon for racial identification to change even among individuals. According to data from a 15-year National Longitudinal Survey of Youth beginning in 1979, a full twenty percent of youths age 14 to 22 experienced a change in their racial identification over the course of the study.[8]

All of these developments contribute to the increasing permeability of racial group identity, leading to a more diverse population less likely to stigmatize and denigrate distinct racial out-groups. They also mark a reality in which identifying cross-racial interests is less about negotiations among distinct, bounded social groups and more about navigating commonalities and differences among friends, family, and loved ones. This is not to disregard the extent to which segregation and racial hostility persist in U.S. communities. However, as intimate interracial relationships increase, the ease with which cross-racial interests can be identified and pursued presumably increases in a roughly comparable measure.

When evaluated in terms of the psychological biases that hamper the politics of privilege, then, the interest convergence approach emerges as a superior alternative. While any attempt to combat social injustice will inevitably run up against psychological and political resistance, an interest convergence approach either avoids activating the most concerning cognitive biases we have discussed or actually takes advantage of them. However, there are still a number of objections to the approach that deserve consideration.

In the first place, emphasizing the intersecting interests of different racial groups might be thought to disregard the genuine differences between those groups and, correspondingly, to underestimate the extent to which the interests of Americans of color might diverge from white interests. Let us discuss this concern about genuinely divergent interests in detail.

* * *

As we have seen, the original analyses of "white skin privilege" and the "wage of whiteness" presuppose that the social privileges offered to white workers are a kind of bribe, ultimately not serving their interests. However, the extensive relative advantages enjoyed by white Americans can certainly *seem* to serve white interests fairly reliably, and a long history of social conflicts that pit whites and people of color against each other can certainly *seem* like they reflect conflicting if not diametrically opposed interests. These conflicts speak to the possibility of what one might call *genuinely divergent interests*: situations where the collective or individual interests of whites really are in fundamental conflict with the collective or individual interests of people of color, situations where no common interest can be identified. Contrary to the idea that white privilege is *merely* psychological, genuinely divergent interests appear to manifest in concrete material inequalities: in health, wealth, education, and more. A skeptic of interest convergence might point out that such inequalities are not contrary to the interests of the whites who benefit from them but are perhaps the result of the instrumentally rational action of the same whites engaging in what sociologist Charles Tilly calls "opportunity hoarding" – the attempt by privileged social groups to control access to resources and opportunities crucial to well-being and to prevent disadvantaged social groups from claiming their fair share of those resources.[9]

The more common these genuinely divergent interests are, the less effective an interest convergence approach might be. Moreover, if it turns out that systematic racial oppression places whites and people of color at odds in ways that tend not to allow for interest convergence, then an approach centered on recognizing and abolishing the privileged position of whites in that system (either by persuasion or by other means) may turn out to be preferable to an interest convergence approach.

The possibility of genuinely divergent racial interests was not lost on the progenitors of interest convergence theory. Bell, who, as we have seen, coined the phrase to explain the advances of the civil rights era, also pointed to the *divergence* of Black and white interests to explain how civil rights legislation was steadily dismantled in the decades following the collapse of the Soviet

Union and the rise of neoliberalism. This is an implication of interest convergence theory that is often misunderstood: the claim that racial justice victories correspond to historical moments of interest convergence means that those victories are especially precarious, prone to reversal as soon as convergent interests diverge, and powerful whites find ways to pursue their own interests without concession to their non-white counterparts.

More recent critical race theorists have also emphasized divergent interests to varying degrees. Ian Haney Lopez, for example, provides a fascinating analysis of the key decisions that shaped the legal definition of whiteness in the U.S. and suggests that such an analysis "demonstrates that when confronted with the falsity of racial lines, many Whites – even those in the highest positions of public trust and under the greatest charge to do justice – will choose to entrench White identity and privilege rather than allow its destabilization."[10] Similarly, in an analysis of *Brown v. Board* near its fiftieth anniversary, Lani Guinier writes that "the apparent interest convergence between northern liberals and southern blacks ultimately perpetuated a more durable divergence of interests within and between the black and white communities."[11]

It is challenging to address the issue of genuinely divergent interests in a general way. Here too, a compelling response requires detailed, domain-specific analyses of the interests at stake in various social conflicts. However, there are a few general points worth emphasizing before turning to such specifics. First, it is important to distinguish between individual and collective interests in order to recognize that at least some cases where interests appear to diverge along racial lines are really more like collective action problems within white communities. Collective action problems arise when the interests of an individual conflict with the interests of a group to which he or she belongs. The so-called "prisoner's dilemma" is a classic if somewhat contrived illustration.

Imagine that two individuals are accused of committing a crime together. They are detained and questioned separately. The interrogating officers explain to each "prisoner" that if he confesses, and his partner does not, then the confessing partner will be released without charges, and the other will receive a three-year prison sentence. If neither partner confesses, then both will receive one-year sentences (on a different, lesser charge). If both partners confess, however, then both will receive two-year sentences.[12]

If we think of the two partners as a collective, and total the prison time for each outcome, the best outcome would be for both to remain silent, and the worst outcome would be for both to confess. However, from the perspective of each prisoner considered individually, the best outcome would obviously be to avoid prison altogether by confessing. What interests scholars about such stylized dilemmas is that by pursuing their individual self-interest, the prisoners' actions actually and predictably lead to a worse outcome for themselves (and, in this case, the worst possible collective outcome).

While the manipulative sort of bargaining reflected by the prisoner's dilemma does have some rough real-world correlates in the world of criminal justice, the broader point of the example has much wider philosophical import, explaining why collective action, even where its benefits are most obvious, can be hard to bring about.

Consider a more realistic and, for my purposes, relevant example. The term "blockbusting" refers to a manipulative strategy where real estate agencies prey upon the racial anxieties of white homeowners and the limited opportunities of prospective homeowners of color. The typical blockbusting scheme weaponizes the relocation of a few families of color into a white neighborhood, aiming to convince white homeowners that the arrival of these families is a harbinger of neighborhood transformation. In light of the allegedly impending transformation, and a corresponding fear of plummeting property values, those white homeowners who are convinced by this strategy will often sell at a loss (or at least for less than fair market value). The blockbusting real estate interests then turn around and market the properties to buyers of color, often at inflated prices, maximizing their profits, and rendering their racial prophecies self-fulfilling.[13]

It is fairly obvious in this case that the interests of neither white residents nor buyers of color are served by such an exploitative (and now illegal) strategy. However, if we think about the situation from the perspective of the white homeowners, and from an amoral perspective of purely financial interest, the situation is somewhat more complex. It is true that it would be best for these white homeowners to collectively resist blockbusting schemes and thereby resist the financial loss of selling their home at a deflated value. However, this interest is served only if all residents act consistently with it. If some do not, the calculation changes for the remaining homeowners. Given that, sadly, the racial diversification of a neighborhood often does result in decreased property values, white homeowners may feel pressured to be among the first, not the last to sell. Indeed, the lack of anticipated solidarity combined with racial and economic anxiety is precisely what makes blockbusting such an effective and profitable strategy.

Collective action problems are challenging, and I won't pretend to provide a definitive solution here. However, it is worth noting that, unlike the prisoner's dilemma, real-world collective action problems generally entail the possibility of communication among parties, and communication has been shown to be effective at inducing the sort of cooperation that neutralizes such problems.[14] Moreover, and more directly to the current point, even if collective action problems are difficult to resolve, this is a different and arguably less difficult problem than the problem of genuinely divergent interests. As with the blockbusting example, many cases of interracial conflict may arise not from divergent interests but rather from collective action problems hampering the successful pursuit of convergent interests. In these cases, communication both within and across racial groups, making collective interests explicit and discussing the ways in which different courses of action might serve or undermine them, is precisely what an interest convergence approach recommends. The politics of privilege offers no corresponding strategy, to address either allegedly divergent interests or collective action problems.

A second response to the objection based on divergent interests relies on the distinction between ultimate and proximate interests. There may be occasions when the proximate interest of a white individual or community becomes opposed to the proximate interest of an individual or community of color, but acting on that proximate interest undermines a shared ultimate interest. For example, it might be in the proximate interest of whites to protect unequal access to higher education, thus securing for themselves the advantages that such education entails and insulating themselves from greater competition for highly skilled, highly compensated careers. However, if such exclusion results in massive non-white unemployment, which in turn results in increases in crime, social spending, and general social malaise, whites' ultimate interest in safe, stable, and sustainable communities might be better served by educational inclusion. Some of the harmful effects of exclusion might be avoided by extreme residential segregation, but that kind of segregation itself undermines shared ultimate interests in political stability, effective democratic governance, and the like.

Finally, and perhaps most importantly, class-blind analyses of white privilege frequently conflate the interests of white *elites* with the interests of white Americans generally. Taiwo's concept of "elite capture," which we encountered in Chapter 1, helps to explain the frequency. While there are certainly some advantages that attach to visible whiteness, which thereby transcend class boundaries, statistical racial inequalities can sometimes conceal the way in which those advantages are distributed and shaped by class status. For example, the shocking and often cited inequalities in wealth between white Americans and Americans of color (especially Black and Hispanic Americans) are dramatically skewed by the wealthiest Americans, who are overwhelmingly white and who control a massive proportion of the country's wealth.[15] By contrast, inequalities between the white working class and working-class Americans of color have narrowed significantly, due to both improving outcomes for the latter and declining outcomes for the former. The result, according to one comprehensive study of American wealth demographics, is that "nonwhite working-class families—those without a four-year college degree—[have] became more similar to working class non-Hispanic whites in terms of family income and wealth."[16] Given this development, speaking generically of white economic interests and contrasting them with the economic interests of Americans of color is likely to be misleading. This is why an intersectional, class-conscious approach to antiracism is preferable to the class-blind politics of privilege and why attempting to articulate and pursue cross-racial class interests is so crucial at this particular historical moment.

Still, despite my overarching emphasis on enrolling the white working class in anti-racist efforts, it is worth noting that an interest convergence approach is not limited to identifying common interests among whites and communities of color, nor does it assume a binary conception of race (despite my occasional reliance on the white/non-white dichotomy). An interest convergence approach can also be effective for identifying and negotiating common interests among Americans of color. Let me expand upon this claim briefly before turning to the discussion of some specific socio-political issues and the cross-racial interests that correspond to them.

* * *

One of the criticisms I have leveled against the politics of privilege is that it focuses too much on white psychological transformation and too little on structural change. If an interest convergence approach were understood too narrowly, as requiring anti-racist work to align with white interests, it might be similarly criticized, if not for emphasizing psychological transformation, at least for objectionably centering white experiences. But such a narrow reading of interest convergence theory is unwise and untenable. Not only does the theory have the potential to engage working-class whites in anti-racist projects, it also provides a framework for thinking about interracial coalitions among people of color.

Such coalitions are not new or theoretical. In a country with a white majority, communities of color have frequently had to form interest-based alliances in order to secure political power or achieve political objectives. Nearly twenty-five years before some would characterize the election of Barack Obama as the long-awaited result of such alliances, Jesse Jackson's "rainbow coalition" formed to address the interests of racial minorities in light of the racially regressive policies of the Ronald Reagan era. While the prospect of a "rainbow coalition," borrowed from the more radical conception of Black Panther party leader Fred Hampton, failed to secure significant structural change, it did lead to Jackson becoming arguably the first Black candidate to be a serious contender for the U.S. presidency. More importantly, this coalitional strategy produced significant local electoral victories, including the election of a wave of Black mayors in large U.S. cities like Chicago and New York. These victories would have been impossible without critical masses of Latino voters joining forces with Black voters to challenge long-standing white domination of city politics.

Electoral politics is an important channel for racial and economic justice, though far from the only one. Coalitions among communities of color have also shaped community organizing and grassroots movements for change.

Lani Guinier and fellow critical race theorist Gerald Torres draw attention to such coalitions with their notion of "political race." Building upon the insight that racialized identities represent "a specific form of public meaning that is tied to the distribution of social goods and is thus intrinsically political," Guinier and Torres argue that racialized groups offer a uniquely illuminating perspective on structural injustices that affect a wide cross-section of society.[17] Thus, they believe that a strategically politicized notion of race offers an effective and inclusive space from which to challenge social injustice generally. The examples they draw upon to illustrate their conception are instructive for thinking about the applications of interest convergence.

One key example invokes the multi-racial alliance that led to the Texas 10 Percent Plan, a unique approach to college admissions devised in the wake of a successful legal attack against affirmative action in higher education. Such an example is especially interesting since affirmative action programs are often described by their critics in terms of racially divergent interests: race-conscious admissions are assumed to provide advantages to certain applicants of color at the expense of white (or, in more recent cases, Asian) applicants. Indeed, this was precisely the argument made by Cheryl Hopwood, a white applicant denied admission to the University of Texas Law School. Her complaint led to one of the earliest successful legal challenges to race-conscious admissions, temporarily prohibiting the use of race as a factor in admissions decisions.[18]

The response to this decision, however, revealed the confusion implicit in the assumption of racially divergent interests. As it turned out, the typical ways in which Texas's most selective universities recruited and admitted applicants disadvantaged many rural white communities as well. Accordingly, a multi-racial coalition of Black, brown, and rural white communities emerged to push for a fairer and more inclusive approach to admissions. The result was the Texas 10 Percent Plan, which guaranteed admission to any student who graduated in the top 10 percent of her high school class. While the success of such an approach continues to be debated, what interested Guinier and Torres was less the result than the process. "By linking the fate of rural and poor whites to that of blacks and Mexican Americans," they argue, "the debate over the Texas 10 Percent Plan revealed that what had been thought of as a racial divide also masked a historic class divide in the provision of elite higher education."[19] While this coalition included working-class whites, by no means did it center them, or develop its strategy based primarily on their interests, as a more cynical understanding of interest convergence might presume.

Many contemporary racial justice issues open up similar spaces for broad interracial mobilization. Even racially specific campaigns, like the Black Lives Matter (BLM) movement, offer such opportunities, despite the efforts of pundits to use them to polarize and manipulate white audiences. In my own mid-sized midwestern city, a local chapter of BLM has led the charge to bring accountability to a police force with a history of systematic racism, brutality, and abuse of power. Shortly after South Bend, Indiana police officers killed Dante Kittrell, a Black man in the grip of a mental health crisis, I found myself in a crowded community center with BLM activists, community members, and representatives of an interfaith organization that has also worked for police accountability. Black community members shared their stories of fear and intimidation, of violence and loss. Soon white folks spoke up as well. Several parents of children on the autism spectrum spoke of their own fears of their children's encounters with police. One man spoke of a brother suffering from addiction and of the indignities and abuses he has suffered at the hands of police. Latino community members spoke of fears of deportation and profiling and added their own stories of violation and abuse.

At a national level, many media outlets noted that the massive uprisings across the country in the wake of the 2020 murder of George Floyd were characterized by significant participation from non-Black Americans, distinguishing them from earlier phases of the movement.[20] It is difficult to determine whether these demonstrators were moved by a sense of moral outrage, a concern for their own interests, or some other reason. Still, one need not betray the critical focus on Black lives, nor deny the disproportionate impact of police brutality on Black communities to appreciate that the movement has created a space for all Americans to re-evaluate the impact of pervasive, racist, largely unaccountable policing in their own lives and communities.

Finally, an interest convergence approach has the advantage of shedding light on the intra-racial dynamics that move racial groups to either support or retreat from racial justice advocacy. This is especially relevant for forms of racialization that group together extremely diverse peoples. The racial/ethnic categories of 'Hispanic' and 'Asian' are notable in this respect, given the diverse range of nationalities, ethnicities, and phenotypes that they pull together under a single racial moniker.[21] For these groups (or at least for some of their members), the racial bribe of white inclusion is not a historical curiosity but a potentially live option for integration. Whether by contrasting an Asian "model minority" to the struggles of a racial underclass or by exploiting the racial-colonial hierarchies internal to Hispanic populations, white supremacist power structures are hard at work attempting to preserve white domination in light of demographic shifts.

The antidote to the attempt to cultivate what Guinier and Torres characterize as "whiteness of a different color" is not to insist upon the immorality of the racial bribe, as the politics of privilege might, but rather to emphasize the crucial interests served by intra-racial solidarity. These interests might be narrowly political, as in the creation of a more powerful voting bloc. They might be economic, as when intra-racial ethnic divisions undermine labor organizing and negotiation. They might be cultural, as when non-native

English speakers band together to resist racist, intolerant language policies. And ultimately, the vast majority of people's interests are aligned with the broad aims of economic fairness, democratic functionality, and survival, which I address in the following chapter.

This suffices to show that the interest convergence approach need not center white interests in its pursuit of racial and economic justice. At any rate, such an approach hardly centers whites more than white privilege discourses, which themselves have been criticized for being a form of white navel gazing that neglects the experiences and effects of racial oppression on people of color.[22]

* * *

The interest convergence approach I have described here has already begun to re-emerge in activist and organizing work and is shaping productive collaborations between academics and changemakers. For example, the Race Class Narrative project, a collaboration among progressive scholars, think tanks, and labor unions, aims to counter right-wing racial scapegoating with messaging that, as the name suggests, emphasizes both race and class. According to its developers, the empirically tested political messaging of the Race Class Narrative "resonates with our base, especially people of color, and brings along the largest possible group of white people on our economic and racial justice policy solutions."[23] By neither shying away from issues of racial justice nor scapegoating or alienating working-class white communities, the Race Class Framework has shown how an intersectional, interest-sensitive approach can successfully combat the racial polarization and manipulation of the Right and its benefactors.

Unfortunately, such an approach remains the exception among academic approaches to racial justice. In this respect, educational institutions and critical pedagogies lag behind their presumed allies in the streets. If such institutions are serious about racial justice, they must move away from the ineffective politics and pedagogy of privilege and adopt approaches that seek to identify and build upon convergent interests. In what follows, I will analyze a few of these interests in greater detail, showing how interracial coalitions might form around three key pillars of well-being: education, housing, and the environment. Happily, these are areas rich with potential for academic and activist collaboration, providing opportunities for educators and intellectuals to move from symbolic to material anti-racism.

Notes

1 Heather McGhee. *The Sum of Us: What Racism Costs Everyone and How We Can Prosper Together* (New York: One World Press, 2021): 23.
2 Derrick A. Bell, Jr. "Brown v. Board of Education and the Interest Convergence Dilemma," *Harvard Law Review*, 93.3 (1980): 518–533.

3 Kwame Ture (formerly Stokely Carmichael) and Charles Hamilton, *Black Power: The Politics of Liberation* (New York: Vintage, 1992): 58.

4 The Combahee River Collective, "The Combahee River Collective Statement," in Barbara Smith, ed. *Home Girls, A Black Feminist Anthology* (Rutgers, NJ: Rutgers University Press, 2000).

5 A.L. Chaikin, and J.M. Darley, "Victim or Perpetrator? Defensive Attribution of Responsibility and the Need for Order and Justice," *Journal of Personality and Social Psychology*, 25.2 (1973): 268–275.

6 See Henri Tafjel, M.G. Billig, R.P. Blundy, and Claude Flament, "Social Categorization and Intergroup Behavior," *European Journal of Social Psychology* 1.2 (1971): 149–177.

7 Richard Alba, *The Great Demographic Illusion: Majority, Minority, and the Expanding American Mainstream* (Princeton, NJ: Princeton University Press, 2020).

8 Andrew M. Penner, and Aliya Saperstein, "Engendering Racial Perceptions: An Intersectional Analysis of How Social Status Shapes Race," *Gender and Society* 27 (2013): 319–343.

9 Charles Tilly, *Durable Inequality* (Berkeley: U of California Press, 1998).

10 Ian Haney Lopez, *White by Law*, 139.

11 Lani Guinier, "From Racial Liberalism to Racial Literacy: Brown v. Board of Education and the Interest-Divergence Dilemma," *Journal of American History* 91.1 (2004): 113.

12 For the sake of the stylized illustration, one must set aside the complexities of actual criminal justice systems, including, obviously, the necessity of a conviction prior to sentencing, and simply imagine that the penalties described will in fact obtain.

13 For an excellent analysis of this strategy and its real-world consequences, see Phillip Andrew Morton's 2014 documentary *Spanish Lake*, which details the racial transformation of the titular St. Louis suburb.

14 See John Orbell et al., "Explaining Discussion-induced Cooperation," *Journal of Personality and Social Psychology* 54 (1988): 811–819.

15 As of 2022, there was only one person of color on the Forbes list of the 50 wealthiest Americans, Taiwanese-American billionaire Jensen Huang. Collectively, the 50 wealthiest Americans control more wealth than the entire bottom 50% of earners.

16 William R. Emmons, Ana H. Kent, and Lowell R. Ricketts, "The Bigger They Are, The Harder They Fall: The Decline of the White Working Class," *The Demographics of Wealth*, Essay No. 3, (2018): 5.

17 Lani Guinier, and Gerald Torres, *The Miner's Canary: Enlisting Race, Resisting Power, Transforming Democracy* (Cambridge, MA: Harvard University Press, 2003): 16.

18 Hopwood v. Texas (1996) was ultimately abrogated by the Supreme Court's *Grutter v. Bollinger* (2003) decision, which in turn was overturned by *Students for Fair Admission vs. Harvard* and *Students for Fair Admission vs UNC* (2023), making creative strategies like Texas' even more important for pursuing educational equity.

19 Guinier and Torres, *The Miner's Canary*, 73.

20 Amanda Barroso, and Rachel Minkin, "Recent Protest Attendees are More Racially and Ethnically Diverse, Younger than Americans Overall," *Pew Research Center*. June 24, 2020.

21 This is not to suggest that Black, or for that matter white racial identity is not similarly diverse, especially when viewed through a global lens. But the brute fact of slavery, along with the longer history of Black and white racialization has rendered these racial groups somewhat more homogenous over time, at least within the United States, and at least compared to the categories discussed above.

22 See, for example, Naomi Zack, *White Privilege and Black Rights: The Injustice of U.S. Police Racial Profiling and Homicide* (Lanham, MD: Rowman and Littlefield, 2015); and Michael Monahan, "The Concept of Privilege: A Critical Appraisal," *South African Journal of Philosophy* 33.1 (2014): 73–83.

23 See https://www.wemakethefuture.us/history-of-the-race-class-narrative. See also their white paper: https://static1.squarespace.com/static/5fd0f29d0d626c5fb471be74/t/6334803965d1a71928bff01b/1664385084488/RCN+Memo.pdf.

5

OUR SCHOOLS, OUR HOMES, OUR PLANET

As I have said above, a thorough defense of the interest convergence approach ought to identify and describe specific areas of interracial interest convergence, especially in those social spheres where interests are commonly thought to diverge along racial lines. That is what I aim to do in this chapter, focusing on three core issues: education, housing, and environmental justice (especially as it has manifested in the fight against climate change). Of course, these issues will look somewhat different in different communities, and so the task of precisely articulating and pursuing convergences of interest is best left to activists and organizers within those communities. That is just to say that pursuing interest convergence is a political rather than theoretical task. Still, the following analyses may provide some useful guidance for those efforts, beyond the abstract defense of interest convergence presented in the previous chapter.

Further, consistent with the insights of the Marxist scholars who first described white skin privilege, these analyses bring the oppositional role of capital into greater relief. That is, it will become clear here (if it is not clear already) that one of the main drivers of racial and economic injustice in each of these spheres is the interest of capital, which exploits racial division in order to privatize, commodify, and extract profit from distinctively human needs and interests. This insight helps us to identify a common foe, which, for better or worse, turns out to be especially conducive to reconstituting the boundaries of groups and group interests. Further, it demonstrates that it is possible (and necessary, in my view) to frame collective resistance to racial and economic injustice in these spheres as an anti-capitalist project. Only in this way can we move beyond feeble and insincere efforts at "inclusion" to genuinely transform the racist and exploitative systems that continue to shape American life.

DOI: 10.4324/9781003461210-6

Education, housing, and environmental justice are by no means the only issues where one might pursue a strategy of interest convergence. But I have chosen these issues because they have historically functioned as pillars of white supremacy in the United States and, as such, are often seen as being structured by white privilege. Here, again, the privilege-centering view is not wrong, per se. But consistent with the general view I have developed in these pages, the value of the privileges enjoyed by working-class whites in each of these arenas has eroded, and this deflation of the "wage" of whiteness opens up opportunities to pursue converging interests.

I have also chosen these issues because they intersect in interesting ways. Given the funding formulas typical in the United States, racial inequality in education is often connected to residential segregation and neighborhood poverty, which, of course, are connected to the issue of safe and affordable housing. The push for safe and affordable housing, in turn, intersects with struggles for environmental justice in communities exposed to dangerous levels of emissions, toxins, and pollutants. Finally, as I argue below, each of these areas represents a critical foundation of democratic life. A functional education system, affordable homes in safe neighborhoods, and, of course, an ecological system that can sustain human life are all crucial preconditions for creating a functional, multiracial, multicultural democracy. Thus, even as we delve into the specifics of each of these issues, the ways in which they point to a common struggle should shine through. Let me begin with the issue of education.

* * *

In the United States, battles for racial justice are frequently fought in the arena of educational policy. It was the struggle for school desegregation and educational equality that jump-started the civil rights movement, creating a legal framework for challenging racial inequity in other spheres. The consequences of this monumental policy shift reverberated for decades, as conflicts over desegregation, busing, district boundaries, and more roiled cities North and South. Within higher education, debates over affirmative action, inclusive curriculum, and more are now nearly as old as *Brown's* desegregation mandate. And more recently, racial politics and education have collided again, as attacks on the alleged influence of critical race theory and other race-conscious pedagogies have turned local school boards into sites of partisan political struggle. Simultaneously, education – specifically, the possession of a four-year degree – has become perhaps the most significant contemporary marker of class difference, carving an especially stark division among white Americans, as we have seen. This rift has led not only to material inequality but also to record levels of distrust of educational institutions among those who are locked out of or underserved by them.

It should not be surprising to find education at the center of race- and class-based conflicts. In societies that employ meritocratic ideologies, education is usually presented as the key to social mobility. Though regularly exaggerated and used to rationalize structural inequalities of opportunity, there is some truth in the view that links education with social mobility, as the data on working-class white Americans show. Perhaps for this reason, education is often understood as a sphere of divergent interests, with white Americans fighting to control access and limit competition for scarce opportunities for social and economic advancement. But this sort of view, while accurately and appropriately directing attention to persistent racial inequalities, can overlook the ways that a broken education system harms nearly everyone, ossifying social hierarchies, ramping up resentment, and ultimately undermining democracy.

As with so many apparently divergent interests, the assumption of scarcity shapes the educational landscape. There is only so much money to be allocated to school systems, only so many spots in a district's "good" schools, only so many applicants admitted to the nation's most selective and prestigious universities. As a result, these resources and opportunities are subject to intense conflict, "hoarded" by families with the power to restrict access and limit competition. Such opportunity hoarding results in massive and well-documented racial inequalities: in spending per pupil, in student achievement, in graduation rates, and more.[1] This might be taken to suggest that white Americans are "winning" the competition for educational dollars and thereby securing a disproportionate share of the rewards of educational achievement.

Here, too, there is some truth but also some potentially lost nuance. To begin with a rather obvious point: the majority non-white schools whose relative disadvantage reveals structural racism at work are also attended by white students, often those from families who cannot afford to "escape" the impoverished neighborhoods and regions the schools serve. This is evident in the history of formal desegregation, where many wealthier white families either moved away from desegregating schools or moved their children into private schools that were legally and economically insulated from integration mandates.[2] For the remaining white students and families, their interests in improving their local schools converge with their neighbors of color. Moreover, as gentrification brings white students and families back into previously distressed urban areas, the quality of the area's schools becomes a potential space for converging interests, though differences in wealth and power have the potential to poison such cooperative endeavors.

Second, while discussions of educational inequality often bring to mind the struggling inner-city school, rural school districts also frequently lag behind their wealthier urban and suburban counterparts. As one study from

Harvard's Kennedy School of Government noted, rural districts, depending on the state, can receive as much as 50 percent less funding from the federal government per student than urban districts.[3] Of course, rural areas can be just as diverse (and just as segregated) as their urban counterparts, so one should be careful about equating 'rural' with 'white' in the way that some employ 'urban' as a coded term for communities of color. Still, the struggles of rural schools are connected to the general malaise of working-class white communities described in earlier chapters. Struggling schools are less likely to produce college-ready graduates and thus more likely to swell the ranks of those demographics prone to "deaths of despair." The similar struggles of urban and rural schools thus reveal potentially convergent interests in bringing equity to school funding formulas and in improving educational outcomes for those who cannot afford to pay for the best private schools or to live in the wealthy communities whose public schools thrive.

Both of these factors – the interests of white students in majority non-white schools and the struggles of rural school districts – are magnified in the American South. This is not a coincidence. Former slave states specifically, consistently rank near the bottom on a variety of educational measures, from per pupil spending, to test scores, to educational attainment. Complex historical factors loom large in any explanation of this fact. To explain the South's lagging educational achievement, one might begin with the plantation owners' resistance to the education of slaves and, after Emancipation, former slaves. One might trace such resistance through the desegregation mandates of the civil rights era and the creation of private "segregation academies" to facilitate the mass exodus of white students from public schools. One might continue to trace such dynamics into the present, as the expiration of the civil rights–era mandates fuels resegregation efforts, and "school choice" movements continue to redirect dollars from racially diverse public schools to disproportionately white private schools. In other words, one might attribute lagging averages to the intentional efforts of whites to limit Black educational achievement. But as much as the history of Southern education can be seen as a case study in white supremacy, it is also true that the majority of white Southerners, especially those who are not wealthy, are not well served by a fragmented and failing public education system.

Mustering empirical evidence for such a claim is admittedly tricky. Since large numbers of Southern white families have abandoned public schooling, the struggles of public schools may not relate directly to their interests. And since uniform, comprehensive assessments of the decentralized patchwork of private schools in the South are difficult to come by, making apples-to-apples comparisons between, say, Southern private schools and Northern public schools is equally difficult. But the gist of the argument is expressed succinctly by former Mississippi Secretary of State Dick Molpus, who noted that "when [limited resources] are divided between black public schools and [private] white academies, both offer substandard education."[4] Even if white private schools outperform their low-performing public counterparts, the real question, unavoidably hypothetical, is whether they would outperform genuinely integrated, fully supported public schools. Here, there is some non-hypothetical evidence that strongly suggests an affirmative answer.

A wealth of post-*Brown* research demonstrates that attending a racially integrated K-12 school has clear academic, occupational, and civic benefits. Educational sociologist Roslyn Mickelson has compiled and contributed to much of this research. The benefits she enumerates include increased test scores in mathematics, science, reading, and language; higher graduation rates; higher college acceptance and completion rates; and higher incomes and occupational achievement. By these metrics, Black students attending integrated schools show the most improvement compared with their peers in segregated schools. But these benefits accrue across all racial groups, including white students. Statistically, white students are academically better served by racially integrated schools than racially segregated ones.[5]

In addition to these academic benefits, racially integrated schools also offer a host of nonacademic advantages, including reduction in prejudice (the well-established effect predicted by the so-called "contact hypothesis"), increased cross-racial trust and friendship, and an "enhanced capacity for navigating multicultural settings."[6] Arguably, these benefits accrue disproportionately to white students, as students of color are more likely to gain many of them simply by living and working in a majority-white society. Some studies are even beginning to discover persistent health benefits associated with integrated schooling.[7]

All of this evidence suggests that segregation comes at a significant cost to white families: both literal, for those who fork over tuition dollars for segregated private schooling, but perhaps more importantly, in terms of missed opportunities to gain skills and knowledge critical to their children's success and mobility in an increasingly diverse society.

This last argument points beyond the instrumental value of education for social mobility and economic success, directing us to the broader function of education in democratic societies. The civic purposes of education were well understood by the nation's founders, who insisted that an educated citizenry was crucial to the success of democracy. Their vision of taxpayer-funded, broadly (though not universally) inclusive public schools came to fruition in fits and starts over a period of centuries. The turn-of-the-twentieth-century progressive era was an especially critical period, and no thinker of the time was a more effective intellectual champion for universal education than philosopher John Dewey. In *Democracy and Education*, Dewey emphasized that the purpose of education is not just the acquisition of specific skills but the integration of individuals into the life of a community. Most narrowly, such an emphasis provides some justification for the connection between schools and neighborhoods. But Dewey's view went beyond this traditional link between individual schools and specific communities, raising the question: what kind of community arises from the effort to create a uniform, inclusive (and largely compulsory) system of public education for a country as large and diverse as the United States? Many of Dewey's initial examples in *Democracy and Education* describe "like-minded," culturally homogenous groups integrating their children into their specific way of life. But, of course, for culturally, racially, and otherwise diverse countries like the United States, no such common culture binds all Americans together, and attempts to impose one usually amount to an oppressive form of assimilationism. Yet far from invalidating Dewey's aims, the diversity that characterizes democratic societies ultimately legitimates and even necessitates his civic-minded approach to education.

Despite his frequent Eurocentrism, Dewey did recognize and appreciate the diversity that forms the backbone of modern democracies. He acknowledges that "such words as 'society' and 'community' are likely to be misleading, for they have a tendency to make us think that there is a single thing corresponding to the single word." He continues,

> As a matter of fact, a modern society is many societies more or less loosely connected... Inside the modern city, in spite of its nominal political unity, there are probably more communities, more differing customs, traditions, aspirations, and forms of government or control, than existed in an entire continent at an earlier epoch.[8]

The critical question here is: what, if anything, "loosely connects" these various communities?

This is one of the most pressing questions in contemporary political theory, with serious practical implications. Political philosopher Will Kymlicka calls integrating a culturally diverse citizenry without cultural erasure "the greatest challenge facing democracies today," a challenge made all the more pressing by growing waves of extreme nationalism.[9] Some hold that a common legal framework is all that is necessary to hold a citizenry together. Others argue that something more is needed, beyond being subject to the same laws. One might expect, for example, that citizens in a democracy will see themselves not as mere subjects of the law but as its authors (in an abstract, if not literal sense), that they will have a basic knowledge and appreciation of the country's history and the constitutional foundations of its legal order, and that they will understand their rights and responsibilities as citizens. One might call this a "culture" of democracy, with the understanding that it is meant to complement rather than supplant the deeper cultural traditions of the diverse range of groups that might subscribe to it.

If this is correct – if some weak civic glue is needed to hold together the diverse groups populating a democracy – then a common system of education would appear critical to imparting the knowledge and values that serve this function. In an era where democracy itself is under threat, education's ability to foster and sustain social cohesion marks perhaps the most critical educational interest shared by all Americans. An institutional failure here would have dire consequences. In the absence of the common foundation that education helps provide, Americans come to define themselves tribally: by political orientation, by geography, by religion, by race. Worse, these tribal identities are often constructed not in light of shared views or experiences but negatively by contrast with those who are viewed as outsiders and enemies. The end point of such a trajectory is no less than societal collapse. Current political polarization and the corresponding tide of journalistic ruminations on whether the United States might be headed for another civil war are sober reminders of this possible future.

Though this kind of polarization often reveals itself *in* disputes about education, the demise of public education is less frequently identified as its precondition. Trends of increasing private school enrollment and homeschooling were supercharged by the Covid-19 pandemic, and while the reasons for this are complex, and the spike perhaps temporary, decreasing faith in public education certainly predates pandemic-era concerns. Privatization, as we have seen, has been a consistent strategy of white families for avoiding racial mixing. And homeschooling, while chosen for a variety of reasons, has increasingly become the arrangement of choice for religious fundamentalists who bemoan the secular nature and allegedly corrupting influence of public education.

It is not a coincidence, then, that Donald Trump selected Betsy DeVos, an unwavering critic of public education to serve as his Secretary of Education, a billionaire who, having never attended a public school herself, has fought unceasingly to redirect public dollars away from public schools, even arguing for the dismantling of the very department she was charged with leading. Critics like her reject the civic goals of education, seeing them as a kind of government indoctrination. They understand education instead as a consumer good, devoid of public purpose. If a family happens to value an emphasis on history, or civic responsibility, or a school's demographic diversity, they are free to seek out (and pay for) such a specialized academy, in the way one searches for a favorite kind of cereal at the grocery store. But if a family is turned off by demographic diversity or would rather instruct their children in Biblical literacy than civic education, then that brand of cereal is on the shelf as well, and the state would be seen as overreaching if it pushed its "consumers" toward another choice.

There is no better recipe than this for creating a fragmented, polarized society where mutual understanding is lost. In the absence of a common framework for truth, society becomes mired in disinformation, unable to sift through an increasingly confusing media landscape. Unaccustomed to encountering those who are different from themselves, its residents are susceptible to efforts to demonize fellow citizens. Eventually, charismatic demagogues exploit these divisions, presenting themselves as the champions of one group, protecting them from the increasing dangers posed by the others. In such a highly charged environment, democracy comes to be seen as an unaffordable luxury, a tradition of "ours" that is being abused by "them," requiring the suspension of normal rights and freedoms, until such dangerous elements can be neutralized.

This is precisely the dynamic that made the Greek philosopher Plato wary of democracy near its inception, more than 2,000 years ago. Democracy, he argued, provides so much freedom, and so little guidance, that its citizenry ends up becoming so diverse as to be incomprehensible to one another. The corresponding emphasis on equality makes qualitative distinctions among ways of life anathema, placing the just and the wicked, the wise and the ignorant, the expert and the novice on equal footing. Such a loosely knit social fabric is easily torn apart by a power-hungry demagogue, who can cleverly manipulate a poorly educated public. Then, like the swing of a pendulum, democracy "produces its opposite," collapsing into tyranny and authoritarianism.

It's tough to find full-fledged defenders of Plato's political theory. His idea of a just society is deeply hierarchical and inegalitarian, envisioning the wisest, most educated citizens, "philosopher kings," ruling over the rest with neither consent nor accountability. But thoughtful defenders of democracy, including, to some extent, the framers of the U.S. Constitution, have almost always considered Plato's criticisms carefully. And it is not lost on any careful reader of Plato's *Republic* that the bulk of the text is dedicated to presenting what amounts to a rigorous and highly structured education system. It is education that is presented as the key to avoiding the kinds of manipulation that precede the worst, most tyrannical organizations of society. Whatever one makes of Plato's aristocratic reproach of democracy, this point has stood the test of time. Even if democracy itself is not destined to collapse into tyranny, an uneducated democracy always runs such a risk.

In light of this risk, the racial divisions and inequalities present in the education system, which may serve the narrow interests of some white communities, ultimately weaken a system essential to democracy. The erosion of the civic core of public education and its replacement by a patchwork "marketplace" of schools and curricula serve no one, save perhaps the handful of profiteers who have used such arrangements to enlarge their fortunes.

It can be difficult to move people to act in pursuit of goals as lofty as democratic flourishing (or to avoid harms as dire and seemingly distant as societal collapse). This is especially so when pursuing such goals entails acting in ways that undermine perceived or short-term interests. But I hope it is now clear that racial segregation and inequality in the U.S. education system, while deeply and intentionally harmful to communities of color, also pose grave threats to white Americans. The structural racism of American schools evolved in step with the "wage of whiteness" strategy, reinforcing alleged white superiority in both form and content. But as in other areas, the value of this aspect of the "wage" has deflated significantly for many whites, especially those of lower socioeconomic status. The resulting educational arrangements, perhaps ironically, have undermined their ability to integrate into an increasingly diverse society, limiting their social and economic success. This, in turn, has led to widespread mistrust and loss of faith in the educational system, further fueling the social fragmentation that precedes democratic decline.

Here, again, I am not attempting to argue that things are *uniquely* bad for working-class whites. The ways in which white supremacy undermines their interests pale in comparison with the harms that such a system has inflicted upon communities of color. But the fact that the system fails to consistently serve white interests complicates simplistic narratives that claim that educational inequalities advantage all white Americans equally and opens up a political space for pursuing converging interests.

Let us now turn to a closely related topic, one which is also frequently assumed to reflect diverging racial interests.

* * *

Like education, housing has long been a key component of the compensatory "wage" of whiteness. When the Great Depression shook the foundations of American capitalism, a crisis of homelessness followed, with more than two million Americans unhoused. Many sought shelter in hastily constructed shanty towns on the outskirts of cities, often referred to as "Hoovervilles," a jab at President Herbert Hoover's perceived responsibility for the dire situation. Hoover's successor, Franklin Delano Roosevelt, inherited the crisis and correspondingly made housing a central focus of New Deal legislation. The result was the creation of the Federal Housing Administration (FHA), which helped create a financing structure that would make mortgages more accessible and affordable for millions of Americans. Yet, through a process known as redlining, the FHA essentially excluded non-white communities from accessing these mortgages.[10] Supported by other racially discriminatory policies, like racial restrictions on home ownership in many neighborhoods, the result was that Americans of color were effectively locked out of homeownership for half a century, denied access to an asset that would become the literal foundation of middle-class security and wealth accumulation.

In addition to federally insuring the private mortgage market, the other arm of New Deal housing policy involved the large-scale construction of public housing. Roosevelt was deeply committed to public housing, viewing it not only as a means of providing a basic human right but also, like public education, as a way of forming good citizens. Thus, the National Housing Act directed substantial funding to the creation of large-scale, government-subsidized housing. Yet, as with low-cost mortgages, public housing was initially rendered inaccessible to families of color. The first public housing projects were for whites only, some even displacing Black communities to make way for the massive construction projects. Eventually, separate facilities were constructed for Black residents but, like most segregated accommodations, they were far inferior to those created for white residents. Over time, as suburban housing and private mortgage funding expanded, white demand for public housing waned. Meanwhile, with Black families having few other paths to affordable housing, Black demand steadily increased. As a result, public housing became disproportionately utilized by Black and other families of color. Neglected, underfunded, and eventually ravaged by epidemics of addiction, HIV, and other social ills, "the projects" gradually became areas of concentrated poverty and crime, such that when the "tough on crime" movement arrived in U.S. politics, they became a central target. The mass demolitions that resulted reflect a commonly held view of public housing as a tried-and-failed approach.

Thus far, we find a familiar pattern of divergence, with policies catering to white Americans and harming Americans of color. But here, too, the political winds have shifted. Owing in part to predatory lending practices that were developed and refined in communities of color, the infrastructure of affordable home financing exploded spectacularly in 2008. In the resulting recession, many Americans found themselves underwater, with a mortgage balance substantially higher than their home value and reduced income with which to pay it. The flood of foreclosures that followed further exacerbated the crisis, producing levels of housing insecurity unparalleled since the Great Depression.

Common wisdom suggests that the recovery from the "Great Recession" of 2008 is more or less complete. Housing prices have largely recovered, and prior to a wave of inflation-taming monetary policy, mortgage rates had dropped to historic lows. But a closer look at the issue from the perspective of people rather than prices paints a rather different picture. Housing insecurity lingers for many and in many parts of the country. Some Americans never recovered from the gut punch of 2008, and some were only beginning to get back on their feet when a global pandemic brought another wave of housing insecurity. The resulting crisis of homelessness, with mass homeless encampments popping up in many American cities, brings to mind Depression-era "Hoovervilles" and paints a stark visual reminder of the lingering effects of the 2008 crash.

One less visible but equally powerful measure of housing insecurity is the number of "cost-burdened" households. A household is considered "cost-burdened" if it spends at least 30% of its overall income on housing-related expenses. If a household spends more than 50% of its income on housing, it is considered "severely cost-burdened." According to a report from Harvard's Joint Center for Housing Studies, over 40% of American renters are at least cost-burdened, and about half of those are severely cost-burdened. A smaller but significant proportion of homeowners, around 20%, are cost-burdened. Combining data for renters and homeowners, we find that about a third of U.S. households are cost-burdened or severely cost-burdened.[11]

Predictably, given the history of U.S. housing policy, Black and Hispanic households are more likely to be cost-burdened – about 10% more likely. And racial inequalities in homeownership rates persist, even as Black and Hispanic households narrowed the gap slightly in recent years. But this leaves tens of millions of white households experiencing cost burden as well. Does the legacy of racially discriminatory housing policy still benefit them, or would they be better served by an inclusive set of policies aiming to secure affordability for all? This is a complex question with implications for whether policy measures should support renters or homeowners, whether development efforts should focus on cities, suburbs, or rural areas, and more. But in spite of this complexity, an uncomplicated truth is emerging: the increasing unaffordability of housing in the United States risks crippling the economic prospects of an entire generation. Thus, working toward affordable and accessible housing is a project ripe for interracial cooperation and interest convergence.

While housing insecurity burdens rural Americans as well, costs have increased most dramatically in urban areas, thus making cities a logical focus of housing-centered organizing efforts. In historically disinvested Black and brown neighborhoods, rising costs are often driven by gentrification: capital-intensive efforts to "revitalize" neighborhoods, which in many ways mark the reversal of the "white flight" characteristic of the immediate post–civil rights era. Gentrification efforts frequently evoke strong resistance from communities of color, with the perception that the gentrifying forces they oppose represent white interests, preferences, and culture. It is true that gentrification typically brings white residents to neighborhoods of color. It is also true that capital-intensive development efforts often displace longtime residents of those neighborhoods and eventually transform the neighborhoods into bland monoliths of corporate culture. But to equate these things with white interests is to miss the fact that white transplants, initially at least, are often motivated by concerns for affordability, a desire to live in a diverse neighborhood and experience the energy of city life, and more and that these interests are distinct from – and often themselves undermined by – the profit-driven motives of gentrifying developers. Appreciating this point helps support another, more controversial one: that the migration patterns characteristic of gentrification, which bring previously segregated groups into greater contact, might also serve to strengthen interracial interest convergence on issues of housing affordability.

Before defending this somewhat counterintuitive point, let me begin by acknowledging the distinct harms of gentrification as it is experienced by communities of color. In her groundbreaking theoretical work on gentrification, philosopher Margaret Kohn describes five distinct harms: homogenization; displacement; exclusion; transformation of public, social, and commercial space; and economic polarization.[12] Yet, as Kohn points out, most of these harms, including homogenization, emerge late in the process of gentrification, in "completely gentrified" as opposed to "incompletely gentrified" neighborhoods.[13] Understanding this distinction requires an investigation of gentrification as a process with identifiable stages.

Sociological accounts of gentrification typically break the process down into four discrete stages. The first stage is characterized by, as Kohn puts it, "an influx of new residents with low financial capital but high cultural capital" – artists, musicians, "bohemians" – cultural refugees fleeing the restrictive norms and expectations of white suburban life.[14] These transplants may target disinvested but historically significant neighborhoods, purchasing and renovating relatively inexpensive housing or renting in inexpensive neighborhoods with easy access to social, cultural, or transportation hubs. This advanced guard of gentrifiers sets the stage for further waves, though it is important to note that at this early stage, while some transformation of social and commercial space may become visible, relatively little displacement, homogenization, or polarization typically occurs, and newcomers live largely within the established parameters of neighborhood life.

In the second stage, these early gentrifiers are joined by more risk-averse middle-class transplants, drawn to the area's emerging hipness and affordability. While these transplants are also joined by "a few perceptive realtors" and "small-scale speculators," gentrification at this stage is still driven by private individuals intending to make a life in the neighborhood.

The third stage of gentrification represents a tipping point, where real estate developers, investors, and speculators, often aided by allies in city governments, eclipse individual transplants as the driving force of gentrification. As early gentrification researcher Phillip Clay puts it, "the first group looks mainly for a place to live and express their life-style. The arrivals in this third stage include increasing numbers of people who see the housing as an investment, in addition to being a place to live."[15] It is in this stage that large-scale "beautification," "urban renewal," and similar euphemistically described projects begin to dramatically reshape the character and physical appearance of the neighborhood. It is also in this stage when real estate prices begin to increase dramatically, leading to the displacement, first, of renters, and eventually of homeowners as well, thus increasingly homogenizing the neighborhood, excluding potential low-income residents, and increasing economic polarization between the wealthier new residents and the remaining old residents.

The fourth stage completes the process, and the neighborhood is now viewed as "safe" (both literally and financially) for middle-class professionals and, increasingly at this stage, members of the "business and managerial classes."

As one can see, the key development in this process occurs between stages two and three, when the interests of individuals seeking housing are eclipsed by the interests of investment capital. These interests are increasingly central not just to the process of gentrification but to the reproduction of capitalism writ large. In his book *Capital City*, Samuel Stein theorizes the rise of the "real estate state, a political formation in which real estate capital has inordinate influence over the shape of our cities, the parameters of our politics, and the lives we lead."[16] Stein links the rise of this political and economic formation to the deindustrialization of advanced capitalist societies. "As the complex process of deindustrialization unfolded," he claims, "real estate went from being a secondary to a primary source of urban capital accumulation."[17] Stein identifies in this shift the "genesis of gentrification in the United States."

Other recent works on gentrification draw similar conclusions. P.E. Moskowitz' *How to Kill a City* explores the common contours of gentrification in four U.S. cities, outlining the ways in which local, state, and federal governments work with developers to extract maximum profits from disinvested urban neighborhoods. In the case of hyper-gentrified cities like New York and San Francisco, Moskowitz argues that this process has become so all-encompassing that it merits the addition of a fifth stage to the standardly accepted four-stage process, where "neighborhoods aren't just more friendly to capital than to people but cease being places to live a normal life, with work and home and school and community spaces, and become luxury commodities."[18] Moskowitz points, as an example, to Manhattan real estate, which has become an investment vehicle for global wealth to the degree that some of the most expensive residences in the borough (and even whole blocks in some areas) lie vacant the majority of the time, acting simply as holdings in an investment portfolio rather than homes in the traditional sense.

To state the obvious, this hyper-commodification of homes and neighborhoods does not serve the interests of the communities of color that it often targets. But neither does it serve the interests of early-stage transplants, who are often themselves displaced by the later, capital-intensive phases of gentrification. Without underestimating the conflict that can arise from early-stage gentrification, fueled by attitudes of superiority and entitlement on the part of "high cultural capital" white residents, it is possible to imagine early-stage gentrifiers finding common cause with long-time residents to effectively resist the exploitative third and fourth waves of capital-intensive gentrification.

That is, it is possible to identify a convergent, cross-racial interest in living in racially diverse, multicultural, democratically organized, and affordable communities, communities that are collectively committed to resisting the exploitative incursions of real estate capital. Far from a utopian fantasy, the current affordability crisis will make forging such interracial interests increasingly necessary.

Since we are exercising our imaginations, let us be bold. In the place of profit-seeking private developers shaping housing "markets" to enlarge their investment portfolios, let us imagine a massive, New Deal–scale investment in public housing. Instead of luxury high rises and corporate coffeehouses popping up in poor Black and brown neighborhoods, imagine new, affordable public housing complexes, spaces that could meet the housing needs of existing residents as well as newcomers. Imagine these complexes including spaces for art collectives, commercial pop-ups and business incubators, small-scale neighborhood history museums, or other spaces driven by community needs and desires. Imagine such complexes having a thoroughly democratic foundation, guided by resident councils instead of unelected bureaucrats, connected to broader, vibrant neighborhood councils, which in turn are connected to city councils and other representative bodies. Imagine these neighborhood-level democratic bodies not just organizing opposition to undemocratic external forces but doing the messy work of integrating new arrivals into community life, facilitating disputes between old and new residents using practices of restorative justice, and *genuinely* revitalizing communities subject to decades of neglect and abuse.

Our imaginings can be augmented with real-world examples. In Europe, where public housing investments have not been hampered to the same degree by structural racism, government-subsidized "social housing" enjoys wide popularity. Vienna's social housing program stands out as an example of what is possible. Vienna's early twentieth-century "municipal socialism" made affordable housing a priority, and the city has rarely wavered from that commitment in the hundred years since. Nearly half of the city's housing stock is owned and controlled by the city; correspondingly, over half of the population lives in government-subsidized housing. The city-owned complexes combine subsidized rental housing, subsidized owner-occupied homes, apartments for refugees, student housing, and more and include the kinds of amenities one might expect to find advertised on the street-level scaffolding of new luxury condominium developments in U.S. cities. Rooftop pools, gardens, restaurants, co-working spaces, even schools are incorporated into the designs of the attractive, well-maintained buildings, which are thoughtfully integrated into the fabric of the city. The units tend to be mixed-income, and costs are restricted to no more than 20%–25% of household wages, ensuring that no resident will be cost-burdened.

Why can't we have these nice things? In large part because the U.S. has, instead of a history of municipal socialism, a history of structural racism and white supremacy. As detailed above, this history has stigmatized public housing to the extent that even our most progressive legislators lack the political imagination to call for expanding investment in this crucial public good. The closest thing, perhaps, is the Green New Deal for Public Housing Act (introduced by senators Bernie Sanders and Alexandria Ocasio-Cortez), which aims to address the many billions of dollars of deferred maintenance on existing public housing by proposing to retrofit existing units with more efficient, carbon-neutral technologies. While such legislation is critical to ensuring that what little public housing stock remains does not fall into further disrepair, the modest aims of the legislation illustrate what little energy exists, even on the progressive Left, for renewed investment in public housing.[19] As of September 2023, the bill has failed to make it out of committee in either the House or Senate, even with these relatively modest aims.

The stigma associated with public housing extends to other forms of housing support as well. Even the market- and landlord-friendly "Section 8" rent voucher program is critically underfunded and underutilized, serving only a small portion of eligible households, who typically spend years on waiting lists before receiving assistance. The failure to competently administer this program would be scandalous if it hampered more popular programs like Social Security or Medicare. But as with other forms of means-tested support, neoliberal ideologues have managed to create such powerful associations between Section 8 and Black recipients that a racist altercation in Texas in which a white woman told a group of Black teens to "go back to your Section 8 homes" could prompt a *Washington Post* analysis of "How Section 8 Became a Racial Slur." As with other public goods, racial division and white hostility poison the well, such that public investment in a widely beneficial program comes to be viewed as a transfer of resources from white communities to communities of color.

Refuting this myth and overcoming the racial divisions that weaken unified demand for affordable housing are crucial to addressing the affordability crisis. While the lingering infrastructure of credit scores, discriminatory lending practices, unethical real estate agencies, and more still provide unjust advantages to whites seeking housing, these advantages are increasingly not enough to address the root causes of housing insecurity for working-class white families. And not even the rankest white supremacists have been so bold (or so clever) as to suggest new mechanisms for ensuring affordability for whites only. Sanctioned and unsanctioned racial violence may work to keep families of color out of white neighborhoods, as it has for centuries. But it is powerless to get working-class white families into those exclusive neighborhoods in the first place. Those families would be far better served by making common cause with families of color and demanding new investments in safe and affordable housing.

The measures I have suggested here amount to a democratizing of the undemocratic, market-controlled distribution of housing. However, we must acknowledge that unrestrained democracy is not an unqualified good. It runs the risk of trampling on the rights of numerical minorities, and in the case of the United States, this equates to the familiar risk of white domination of putatively democratic institutions. But rights-sensitive forms of democracy remain a far superior alternative to undemocratic market forces when it comes to ensuring the basic right of safe, affordable housing. Organizing across racial lines, especially in gentrifying cities and suburbs, will be crucial to restraining the colonizing forces of capital, which have eagerly turned to real estate as a tool for accumulating and concentrating wealth. Fighting these battles where we live is not only necessary to secure our right to housing and to protect our communities from corporate plunder; it also serves to forge residents in the fires of democratic life, developing and reinforcing the sorts of skills required for living in diverse, multiracial democracies. Like universal education, safe and affordable housing represents a crucial interest for Americans of all races and a building block upon which further interracial solidarity and community might be developed.

* * *

Both affordable housing and accessible, high-quality education have been central to the compensation strategy W. E. B. Du Bois named the "wage of whiteness." But as capitalism has expanded beyond its traditional forms of production and accumulation, the sorts of exploitation that the wage aims to compensate for have expanded as well, creeping into and commodifying previously protected spheres of life, including education and housing. This is fairly obvious in the latter case, as housing in the U.S. has always been market-driven, the brief mid-century push for public housing notwithstanding. Still, at the height of industrial capitalism, the owners of industry could often be relied on to support (and, in some cases, even construct) affordable housing for their workers, as lower housing costs meant that there would be less pressure on them to increase wages. Those days are long gone, however, as the power of developers and real estate capital has increased alongside industry's decreased presence and interest in U.S. city centers.

The commodification of education is perhaps less obvious given the county's relatively robust support of government-subsidized public schooling. But the trend is visible there too, as the privatization movement, bolstered by the neoliberal ideology of "choice," increasingly seeks to monetize the racial divisions that drive white families to abandon public schools. The result, as we have seen, is a fragmented and underfunded education system failing all but the wealthiest Americans. Thus, in both cases, we can see the expanding interests of capital driving the devaluation of white privilege. This is a logical consequence of capital's expansion beyond traditional production. Just as the pressure to reduce literal wages is a well-known feature of capitalism, the devaluation of the metaphorical wage of whiteness is a predictable consequence of capital's expansion into social spheres long structured by racial privilege. Capital is no longer satiated by the hyper-exploitation of racially disadvantaged populations, alongside the purely economic exploitation of racially advantaged populations. As Nancy Fraser observes, capital has an inherent tendency to "cannibalize" its social preconditions, seeking to monetize and capture potential profits wherever they might be found.[20] It is no surprise, then, that social institutions and spheres of life shaped by privilege have been gradually eroded by capital's commodifying tendencies. Nearly a hundred years after Du Bois noted the role of white privilege in fortifying capitalism in an unstable, war-torn nation, the forces of capital now see the price of white privilege as too expensive, the possible returns on expanded white exploitation too tempting, to continue to fully honor the racist bargain.

Nowhere is this more apparent than in the ravaging of planetary resources and the environmental destruction that it has wrought. Centuries of fossil-fueled industrial capitalism have put the planet on the brink of ecological catastrophe. Warming temperatures, leading to rising ocean levels, mass extinctions, extreme weather events, and more, threaten the very survival of the human species. So says the Intergovernmental Panel on Climate Change, a United Nations (UN) body composed of hundreds of climate scientists from 195 member nations. Lobbied extensively by corporate interests and often criticized for understating the risks of climate change, the organization's recent reports are nonetheless increasingly dire. The 2022 summary report, for example, notes the current "widespread adverse impacts and related losses and damages to nature and people," adding that some of these impacts have become irreversible, as "natural and human systems are pushed beyond their ability to adapt."[21] The future looks even more grim, as a consensus emerges among scientists and policymakers that there is "no credible path" to limiting global warming to 1.5 degrees Celsius, the level at which warming begins to produce increasingly catastrophic consequences. To the contrary, a 2022 UN Environment Programme report predicted that, on our current track, the world will see temperatures rise between 2.4 and 2.6 degrees Celsius by the end of the century, a result that would threaten human civilization itself, producing famine, mass migration, extreme poverty, political destabilization, war, and mass mortality.[22]

The worst effects of climate change and environmental destruction more generally tend to be borne by the most vulnerable human communities. Globally, this means that the poorest countries will bear the brunt of climate-related harm although wealthy, industrialized countries have largely created the problem by burning a disproportionate share of fossil fuels. Within those wealthy countries, it means that environmental harms will concentrate in poor and working-class communities and communities of color. This is the defining insight of movements for environmental justice, which have drawn compelling links between human-centered concerns for social justice and concerns for the natural environment.

Here, again, we can easily identify racially divergent interests, in the form of a "not in my back yard" politics that protects white communities from the harmful by-products of their consumption-heavy lifestyles, saddling communities of color with their waste. But ecological systems are superbly disrespectful of political and racial geography, and it is becoming increasingly clear that it is not possible to confine the harmful effects of environmental destruction to poor, racialized, and disenfranchised communities. The dismissively described "externalities" of the relentless production and consumption patterns characteristic of capitalist societies are rendering the planet uninhabitable. Perhaps the world's wealthiest individuals will find creative, tech-savvy ways to insulate themselves from such harms – an interplanetary migration of billionaires, perhaps. But for the rest of us, taking the necessary steps to curb climate change is possibly the most compelling convergence of interest imaginable. What has prevented such a convergence around issues of environmental concern? The answer points again to the misanthropic tendencies of global capitalism.

Many may be surprised to learn that, well before the birth of the IPCC, one of the earliest efforts to understand climate change came from the giant oil company Exxon (predecessor of ExxonMobil). In the mid-1970s, among the first whispers about the warming effects of burning fossil fuels, Exxon initiated a number of studies of the phenomenon, some internal and some in collaboration with university researchers. Far from a corporate hack job, Exxon's efforts were described by those familiar with them as being "at the cutting edge of emerging climate research."[23] The initial conclusions of its research were clear; in 1977, James Black, one of Exxon's lead scientists, wrote an internal memo to the company's executives, stating that "there is general scientific agreement that the most likely manner in which mankind is influencing the global climate is through carbon dioxide release from the burning of fossil fuels." This, of course, was not welcome news for one of the world's largest oil and gas corporations. Worse, Black insisted upon a short time frame – five to ten years – before "hard decisions" would need to be made regarding humanity's continued use of fossil fuels.[24]

If corporations had souls, one might expect that this revelation would have marked the beginning of some serious soul searching within Exxon or at least some old-fashioned "innovation," allegedly the cardinal virtue of the for-profit corporation. Instead, Exxon launched a multi-decade disinformation campaign, funneling tens of millions of dollars into climate change denialism, lobbying against fossil fuel industry regulations, even convincing the U.S. government not to sign on to the Kyoto Protocol and other international agreements to reduce emissions. Other fossil fuel corporations followed their lead and joined their efforts. In 1998, Exxon formed the Global Climate Science Team, alongside its industry competitors and its loyal climate "researchers." The mission of that organization was encapsulated succinctly by an internal memo leaked to the *New York Times*: "victory will be achieved when average citizens 'understand' (recognize) uncertainties in climate science" and when "recognition of uncertainty becomes part of the 'conventional wisdom'."[25]

Given the substantial number of Americans who express uncertainty about climate change, this goal appears to have been attained. A 2019 Pew survey found that only 49% of Americans think that human activity contributes "a great deal" to climate change. The remaining responses split roughly between the belief that human activity plays "some role" in climate change (30%) and the view that human activity contributes "not too much" or "not at all" to climate change (20%). Of those who remain skeptical of the role of human activity in causing climate change, most imagine that "natural patterns in the Earth's environment" are the primary cause of warming temperatures (35% of all respondents), precisely mirroring the disinformation campaigns of Exxon and its collaborators. Predictably, these skeptics are largely unsupportive of political efforts to curb climate change, viewing them as "hurting the economy" and "doing more harm than good."[26]

As with many aspects of American life, beliefs about the changing climate are sharply polarized, with Republicans far less likely to accept the reality of human-caused climate change than Democrats. But there is also a racial dimension to climate denialism, with white Americans about twice as likely to be doubtful or dismissive of global warming than Americans of color.[27] This might be attributed to the fact, noted above, that Americans of color are more likely to have firsthand experience of the harmful effects of a changing climate. It might thus be tempting to see the disproportionate lack of concern among white respondents as a manifestation of white privilege. But the "privilege" of ignoring climate catastrophe is, of course, self-defeating. To imagine that a system that steers humanity ever closer to ecological collapse advantages white communities in any ultimate sense is to miss the forest for the trees. Just as plantation capitalism used the racial bribe of whiteness to gain the allegiance of working-class whites (who gained little economic benefit from slavery), so the fossil fuel capitalists of the late twentieth and early twenty-first century manipulate conservative whites into resisting efforts to address a climate crisis that will inevitably harm them along with everyone else.

At least one study has documented the underappreciated racial dimension of climate attitudes, noting that white racial resentment is highly correlated with climate change skepticism, even after controlling for political party.[28]

Heather McGhee discusses this research in response to a pointed question: "are powerful interests using race to sell climate denialism to white people?" McGhee defends an affirmative answer, noting that "the racial divide on support for climate change action sharpened as Barack Obama made it a priority" and that "by the 2016 election, the coal miner had become a symbol of white masculinity under attack."[29] McGhee's provocative question points us in the right direction, but as a philosopher, I can't resist the urge to make the question more precise. It is not vaguely "powerful interests" that are engaged in racial scapegoating and manipulation but the ideological forces of global capitalism specifically. And as her insight into the racial (and gendered) symbolism of the coal miner suggests, it is not "white people" generally that these ideologues target, but the white working class specifically. As in past eras, when the forces of capital need to shore up the support (or resistance) of the white working class, they return to the bountiful and reliable well of white racial resentment.

It is no surprise that fossil fuel corporations like Exxon would engage in such ideological efforts. An analysis by the Carbon Disclosure Project revealed that, between 1988 and 2015, over 70% of greenhouse gas emissions came from just 100 corporations, with state-owned or multinational oil, gas, and coal corporations comprising the top ten worst offenders.[30] This suggests that, alongside the more nefarious disinformation campaigns of these companies, their efforts to shift responsibility to individual consumers, urging them to reduce their "carbon footprint" through lifestyle changes, constitutes yet another ideological distortion. Still, placing all of the blame on fossil fuel corporations would be short-sighted. The destructive excesses of the fossil fuel industry are not exceptions to some green-able rule of capitalist production. Rather, these companies represent the near-literal engine of global capitalism, fueling the ever-expanding consumption that the system requires.

To begin to understand capitalism's ecologically destructive tendencies, we must understand the way that it conceives of nature itself as an "externality" – not something with inherent value but a "raw material" whose value registers only once it has been transformed into an economically calculable resource. Combined with capitalism's characteristic growth imperative – the idea, for example, that a "healthy" economy is one that expands by a mathematically unsustainable 3%–4% a year – this is a recipe for ecological catastrophe. Fraser echoes this point, claiming that its profit-maximizing imperative combined with its impoverished and self-serving conception of nature creates a "built-in tendency to ecological crisis," such that "capitalism's economy is always on the verge of destabilizing its own ecological conditions of possibility."[31]

This provides us with perhaps the clearest example yet that the relative advantages capital has used to bribe white workers into supporting its imperatives pale in comparison with the damages that continue to accumulate.

While these damages may initially sharpen racial and economic inequalities (especially globally), it is increasingly apparent that virtually no one will emerge unscathed. Here, again, the politics of privilege is ill equipped to fully capture what is at stake. Only by appreciating the ways in which our most basic interests are threatened by the voracious appetites of capital do we stand a chance of mustering a mass movement with the potential to redirect its depressingly predictable, steadily advancing march toward disaster.

* * *

In this chapter, I have briefly sketched the form that an interest convergence approach might take in three core areas of contemporary life: education, housing, and our relationship with the natural environment. While these are spheres undeniably shaped by racial inequality (and thus manifesting white privilege if we were to remain within the paradigm of privilege politics), they are also areas ripe for identifying converging interests across racial groups. By emphasizing the ways in which capitalism creates, manipulates, and exploits racial divisions, I locate my analysis within the growing work on "racial capitalism."[32] Returning to the insights of the most promising elements of Black radical and Marxist traditions, these analyses foreground the ways in which racialization and the specifically racial forms of exploitation that proceed from it are driven by the interests of capital. Importantly, they do this without reducing all conflict to class conflict or distorting the complex, evolving mechanisms of racial oppression to fit nineteenth-century Marxist orthodoxies.

Although notions of white privilege emerged alongside such analyses, the capture and neutralization of the concept that I have traced in previous chapters make it ill suited to understanding, resisting, and transcending the forms of exploitation and oppression distinctive of racial capitalism today. An interest convergence approach, as described in the preceding pages, is a far better fit. To effectively combat the weaponization of racial division that undergirds and sustains racial capitalism, we must forge new interracial alliances, identifying the specific ways that racial capitalism undermines important, widely shared interests: interests in human development, in functional democracy, in breathable air and drinkable water, and, above all, in a world that we can hand down to our descendants without fear or shame.

Pursuing racial and economic justice with these shared interests in mind moves us away from the liberal individualism of the politics of privilege, with its corresponding focus on white moral and psychological conversion. Still, it is not wrong to assume that social transformation entails – perhaps even requires – significant shifts in individual consciousness and public morality. With this in mind, I conclude, in the following chapter, with some further reflections on the relationship between social transformation and the ethical-political consciousness of individuals.

Notes

1 For an overview of some of these trends, see Cristobal de Brey et al., "Status and Trends in the Education of Racial and Ethnic Groups 2018," (NCES 2019-038). U.S. Department of Education. Washington, DC: National Center for Education Statistics. Retrieved April 19, 2023 from https://nces.ed.gov/pubsearch/.

2 This is also why the debate over "school choice" and the increasing privatization of schools is racially charged. It is essentially an attempt to transfer public funds to families who wish to opt out of increasingly diverse public schools, and can thereby be understood as a measure to extend a key advantage of whiteness to those who might be on its economic margins.

3 David Gutierrez, "Little School on the Prairie: The Overlooked Plight of Rural Education," *Harvard Political Review*. February 10, 2016.

4 Sarah Carr, "In Southern Towns 'Segregation Academies are Still Going Strong," *The Atlantic*. December 13, 2012.

5 See Rosyln Mickelson, "Twenty-first Century Social Science on School Racial Diversity and Educational Outcomes," *Ohio State Law Journal* 69 (2008): 1173–1128.

6 See Roslyn Mickelson, "School Integration and K-12 Outcomes: An Updated Quick Synthesis of the Social Science Evidence," *The National Coalition on School Diversity*, Brief no. 5 (October 2016).

7 R.A. Hahn, *Racial and Ethnic Segregation as a Core Social Determinant of Public Health and Health Equity: A Persistent Public Health Challenge in the United States*. Unpublished Manuscript, Center for Surveillance, Epidemiology and Laboratory Services E-69, Centers for Disease Control and Prevention, Atlanta, Georgia 30333.

8 John Dewey, *Democracy and Education: An Introduction to the Philosophy of Education* (New York: The Free Press, 1944): 20-21.

9 Will Kymlicka, *Multicultural Citizenship* (Oxford, Oxford University Press, 1995).

10 See Richard Rothstein, *The Color of Law: A Forgotten History of How Our Government Segregated America* (New York: Norton, 2018).

11 See *The State of the Nation's Housing 2022*. Joint Center for Housing Studies of Harvard University (2022).

12 Margaret Kohn, *The Death and Life of the Urban Commonwealth* (Oxford: Oxford University Press, 2016): 90.

13 Ibid, 107.

14 Ibid, 89.

15 Phillip Clay, and Timothy Pattison, "The Process of Neighborhood Upgrading and Gentrification" (Master's Thesis, Massachusetts Institute of Technology, 1977): 58.

16 Samuel Stein, *Capital City: Gentrification and the Real Estate State* (London: Verso, 2019): 5.

17 Ibid, 45.

18 P.E. Moskowitz, *How to Kill a City: Gentrification, Inequality, and the Fight for the Neighborhood* (New York: Nation Books, 2018): 34.

19 In fairness, the bill does propose to repeal the 1998 Faircloth Amendment, which essentially prohibited the construction of new public housing beyond the number of units that existed at the time of the legislation. Repealing this amendment would be a first step toward pursuing new construction of public housing.

20 Nancy Fraser, *Cannibal Capitalism: How Our System is Devouring Democracy, Care, and the Planet – And What We Can Do About It* (London: Verso, 2022).

21 IPCC Summary for Policymakers, in: *Climate Change 2022: Impacts, Adaptation and Vulnerability. Contribution of Working Group II to the Sixth Assessment*

Report of the Intergovernmental Panel on Climate Change (Cambridge: Cambridge University Press): 9.

22 United Nations Environment Programme. Emissions Gap Report 2022: The Closing Window — Climate Crisis Calls for Rapid Transformation of Societies. Nairobi. https://www.unep.org/emissions-gap-report-2022.

23 Lisa Song, Neela Banerjee, and David Hasemyer, "Exxon Confirmed Global Warming Consensus in 1982 with In-House Climate Models," *Inside Climate News*. September 22, 2015.

24 Shannon Hall, "Exxon Knew About Climate Change Almost 40 Years Ago," *Scientific American*. October 26, 2015.

25 For a discussion of the leak and its contents, see Union of Concerned Scientists, *Smoke, Mirrors & Hot Air: How ExxonMobil Uses Big Tobacco's Tactics to Manufacture Uncertainty on Climate Science*. (Cambridge, MA: Union of Concerned Scientists, 2007).

26 Pew Research Center, "U.S. Public Views on Climate and Energy." November, 2019.

27 M. Ballew et al., "Which Racial/Ethnic Groups Care Most About Climate Change?" (New Haven, CT: Yale Program on Climate Change Communication, 2020).

28 See Salil D. Benegal, "The Spillover of Race and Racial Attitudes into Public Opinion about Climate Change," *Environmental Politics* 27.4 (2018): 733–756.

29 McGhee, *The Sum of Us*, 199–200.

30 Paul Griffin et al., *The Carbon Majors Database: Methodology Report* (London: CDP Worldwide, 2017).

31 Fraser, *Cannibal Capitalism*, 78.

32 See Gargi Bhattacharrya, *Rethinking Racial Capitalism: Questions of Reproduction and Survival* (New York: Rowman and Littlefield, 2018); Susan Koshy, Lisa Marie Cacho, Jodi A. Bryd, and Brian Jordan Jefferson, eds. *Colonial Racial Capitalism* (Durham, NC: Duke University Press, 2022) along with what is arguably the classic source of the concept, Cedric J. Robinson, *Black Marxism: The Making of the Black Radical Tradition*. 3rd ed. (Chapel Hill: University of North Carolina Press, 2021).

6

MORALITY, SELF-INTEREST, AND SOCIAL CHANGE

A Philosophical Detour

Throughout this book, I have developed a critique of privilege-based approaches to anti-racism, based on the claim that these approaches, in their contemporary form at least, fail to transcend the liberal emphasis on white moral and psychological transformation. Instead of speaking to the concrete self-interest of white communities, privilege politics operates in a moral register, telling white Americans that structural racism provides them with unjust advantages and, in the same breath, that morality requires them to resist or reject such advantages. I have argued that such an approach runs aground against powerful psychological biases and that it is ill equipped to motivate necessary structural transformation. But there are some philosophical assumptions and questions here about the relationship between morality, self-interest, and social change that are worth examining more closely. For one, are morality and self-interest really opposed in the way that my argument seems to suggest? If not, then perhaps my critique of the moralizing tone of privilege politics is somewhat lacking in nuance. Secondly, does social transformation require or proceed from moral transformation? Periods of social transformation are often accompanied by shifts in moral understanding. But whether these shifts drive social change or are a result of it (or are, perhaps, correlated in some more complex way) remains an open question. This makes further reflections on the relationship between morality and politics (in the broadest sense) worthwhile.

In this final chapter, I will offer some modest and necessarily limited reflections on these perennial questions. Without attempting to nail down a precise causal relationship between morality and social transformation, I will argue that individual morality and institutional justice are mutually constitutive. This argument builds upon the "virtue ethics" of pre-modern philosophers like Plato and Aristotle and challenges modern theories that understand

DOI: 10.4324/9781003461210-7

morality primarily in terms of decision procedures. Like its predecessors, it acknowledges that morality is not opposed to self-interest, though it avoids the liberal mistake of seeing politics as a simple extension of self-interested concerns for a narrow set of basic rights.

* * *

Questions about the relationship between morality and self-interest have occupied philosophers since the birth of the discipline. Ancient philosophers like Plato and Aristotle saw virtuous activity as a reliable path to happiness and thus as consistent with the self-interest of individual moral agents. Some modern philosophers have followed the ancients in this respect, linking morality to happiness (though in very different ways). Others, like the influential German philosopher Immanuel Kant, saw self-interest as the most significant obstacle to living a morally upstanding life.

Kant's *Grounding for the Metaphysics of Morals*, a staple of introductory ethics courses, paints a stark picture of the opposition between morality and self-interest or at least between morality and "inclination" – what we ought to do versus what we want to do. He surmises that "man feels within himself a powerful counterweight to all the commands of duty…this counterweight consists of his needs and inclinations, whose total satisfaction is summed up under the name of happiness."[1]

The position makes some intuitive sense. If morality did align with our happiness in the way that some ancient philosophers supposed, it would be hard to explain why anyone ever acts immorally. After all, who would knowingly act in such a way as to undermine their own happiness? Rather, when people commit immoral acts, it makes sense to assume that their preferences (and so, on at least one kind of account, their happiness) incline them toward something contrary to their moral duty. If I find a wallet full of cash lying on the ground, I would certainly be inclined to keep it, and doing so would likely be in my financial self-interest as well. At the same time, I might recognize that, in spite of my inclinations, attempting to return the wallet (and the cash) to its rightful owner would be the right thing to do.

Beyond such simple, context-free examples, though, Kant's moral theory quickly encounters its own challenges and counterintuitive results. If the dictates of morality categorically conflict with the needs, inclinations, and interests of its human subjects, then it would appear that humanity is doomed to be immoral. On a strong deterministic view, in which our evolved instincts and psychological inclinations fully dictate our actions, Kantian morality would be, strictly speaking, impossible. But even on a non-deterministic view, in which human freedom is taken to entail our ability to act contrary to our inclinations, the conflict between morality and inclination would still presumably render such actions rare, marking a level of moral development that most of us never reach.

Either way, one wonders about the practical use such a moral theory, beyond offering a pseudo-secular explanation of the inherent sinfulness of humanity. (Indeed, contrary to Kant's reputation as a secular Enlightenment philosopher, his thought is deeply indebted to the Pietist theological tradition of his time, and he takes great pains to make his philosophical conclusions consistent with key Christian doctrines, including the idea of Original Sin.) If truly moral action is either impossible or exceptional, then moral persuasion is unlikely to be an effective means of building a political movement with the capacity to transform racial capitalism and white supremacy. Indeed, it is unlikely to be an effective means of doing much of anything, aside from occupying the intellectual energies of academic philosophers and filling the copious pages of academic journals.

This inefficacy is closely related to what philosophers and moral psychologists call the problem of moral motivation. Even if human beings are capable of rationally understanding which actions are right or wrong, it doesn't follow that we will be motivated to act on that understanding. It may be that moral understanding is a primarily intellectual endeavor, while moral motivation has more to do with non-cognitive features of human psychology – our emotions and desires. Some philosophers, drawing from a tradition of moral skeptics like Friedrich Nietzsche and David Hume, have gone so far as to suggest that morality is essentially a kind of self-deception, in which humans attempt to rationalize doing what our instincts, desires, or emotions drive us to do, or justify our failure to do what, at an intellectual level, we know we should.

Interestingly, this sort of self-deception is viewed by some as central to the forms of racism that drove European colonialism and racial exploitation. David Livingston Smith, for example, argues that it is humanity's capacity for self-deception that allows us to be ethically inclined (empathetic, cooperative, and kind) toward our "friends" and brutally unethical (violent, exploitative, and indifferent) toward our "enemies." The key to this kind of self-deception, according to Smith, is dehumanization. By convincing ourselves that our "enemies" lack the essential human qualities that ground moral standing, we can act toward them with impunity, simultaneously insulating our moral understandings from any cognitive dissonance.[2] When ingroups and out-groups get defined by allegedly immutable characteristics like race, the results are particularly horrific.

Among its other insights, Smith's analysis illuminates one of the great hypocrisies of human history: that Europe could develop the lofty moral ideals of freedom, equality, and democracy characteristic of its Enlightenment period alongside the brutal colonization, enslavement, and expropriation of non-European peoples. Viewed through the lens of self-deception, this tension is less mysterious. As philosopher Charles Mills quipped, "European humanism usually meant that only Europeans were human."[3]

Beyond its historical applications, self-deception of this kind seems to present a serious obstacle to the interracial solidarity to which an interest convergence approach is committed. It is surely part of the story of why the white working class would so readily accept a racial bribe that sacrifices their ultimate interests for proximate gains and relative advantages.

But we should not be too quick to dismiss morality as simply a form of self-deception, nor as mere bourgeois ideology, as some orthodox Marxists have. As the U.S. culture wars have demonstrated, moral claims and arguments that evoke "values" can be quite effective at reshaping political identities, even where those claims and arguments barely conceal raw racial resentments simmering underneath the surface. It would be foolish for progressive social movements to reject such approaches, even if we reject the broader view of social change as entailing a kind of mass moral conversion.

Even for Kant, the relationship between morally pure and self-interested motives is primarily an epistemological problem. That is, it has to do with whether we can know for certain that a person's motive is purely moral, not whether a right action can simultaneously be one that we are inclined toward or one that serves our self-interest. Empirically, Kant acknowledges that many (perhaps most) morally desirable actions coincide with actions we might take for self-interested reasons. "To preserve one's life," he claims, "is a duty; and furthermore, everyone has also an immediate inclination to do so."[4] Similarly, he describes a duty of beneficence (being kind, roughly) and a duty to "secure one's own happiness" as duties to which most of us are also naturally inclined. The distinction he lands on, then, is not a distinction between duty and self-interest but a distinction between actions done "in accordance with" duty and actions done *solely from* a sense of duty.

While such a distinction might be important for understanding the deep theoretical foundations of morality, it is decidedly less so for those wishing to employ moral persuasion in the pursuit of social transformation. That acting morally is consistent with acting in one's own interest means there is no contradiction in a pluralistic strategy that aims to articulate common interests as well as identify shared values and moral commitments.

Secondly, the long-standing distinction between reason and emotion, on which the problem of moral motivation as well as the views of various moral skeptics rely, turns out to be complicated by advancements in cognitive psychology. In a critique of Jorge Garcia's "volitional" conception of racism – one in which racism is viewed as a non-rational vice centered in the "heart" rather than the head – Charles Mills points out that "the traditional sharp polarization within philosophy of emotions vs. rationality, the heart vs. the head, has long since been superseded…judged to be misleading because emotions are tied *to* perceptions, conscious or unconscious, which can be translated into beliefs."[5] In the context of racism, this means that negative feelings toward racial out-groups – hatred, perhaps, or disgust – are typically tied to beliefs about what members of those groups are like. More generally, it means that we cannot divorce our rational judgments about what we ought to do from our inclinations and feelings about our doing it.

Here, too, this may be a problem for Kantian moral theory, but it is less worrisome for concrete practices of moral persuasion. Some years ago, a Los Angeles-based activist group drew national attention for its claim that its innovative canvassing technique could change people's minds about supporting ballot initiatives that discriminated against the LGBTQ community, simply by having a short conversation with a gay or lesbian canvasser. The key, the organization claimed, was that by activating humans' powerful capacity for empathy – by getting them to see the world through the eyes of their canvasser – radical shifts in belief were possible, even likely. This result flew in the face of the commonly accepted wisdom of political analysts, which held that people's beliefs about such issues were stubbornly intractable. In 2014, the organization's findings were published in the prestigious academic journal *Science*, bolstering the group's claims with compelling data.

Unfortunately, the article was later retracted, based on allegations that its authors falsified data and misrepresented some aspects of their methodology. But the method was eventually redeemed when other activists and researchers were able to replicate the original study's findings.[6] Organizers have found significant success applying this empathy-building form of deep canvassing to other areas, including abortion rights and police reform, as well as building support for specific political candidates. A recent study has further noted the technique's potential to address political polarization, using empathy-building prompts to reduce partisan animosity and increase openness to considering opposing viewpoints.[7]

The key lesson here is that, despite the common refrain that Americans are immovably polarized and irrationally persistent in their moral and political views, the method of "active perspective taking" is surprisingly effective at shifting political views, because it aims to solicit empathy rather than pursue a purely intellectual form of persuasion. Much to the chagrin of moral philosophers, there is no guarantee that empathy-primed individuals will shift their views in the right direction, though. The activation of empathy, in other words, might be used as readily for regressive causes as for progressive ones (or false moral claims versus true ones, if one is committed to moral objectivity). Still, these findings show us that emotion is not a liability for moral discourse or movement building. Rather, under the right conditions, it can be a resource.

In short, both the opposition of morality and self-interest and the related juxtaposition of moral reasoning with allegedly irrational emotions and desires turn out to be overly simplistic and difficult to defend. This suggests that a politics oriented to identifying and pursuing overlapping interests need not eschew morality entirely and that moral persuasion, to be effective, might invoke "passions" like empathy as well as instrumentally rational calculations of interest. Still, such conclusions do not entail the stronger causal claim that social transformation is *caused* by the collective moral transformation of society or of a given demographic. Therefore, it should not be taken to invalidate the criticism of approaches (like the politics of privilege) that focus their efforts almost entirely on white moral and psychological transformation, assuming social change will inevitably follow. To further defend this claim, let me now turn to the discussion of the relationship between morality and social change.

* * *

When we hear the word 'justice' today, we are immediately inclined to think in terms of systems and institutions. That is, we think of justice as applying to the structure of society as a whole or to the organization of government, the economy, and so on. Systems that are fair and well ordered are deemed just, while those that are unfair and disordered are deemed unjust. By contrast, 'morality' or 'ethics' usually evokes the internal conscience of an individual struggling with right and wrong, good and bad, virtue and vice.[8] However, this distinction between justice and morality may have seemed strange to pre-modern thinkers, many of whom were perfectly comfortable speaking of 'justice' as an individual virtue.

Plato's *Republic*, for example, begins with an analysis of the "just person," viewing justice as a virtue exercised in such putatively admirable actions as "telling the truth" and "paying one's debts." But this discussion is quickly derailed, descending into a long inquiry into whether justice of this sort is actually desirable or beneficial. This leads Socrates, Plato's protagonist, to shift the scope of the analysis:

> We say, don't we, that there is the justice of a single man and also the justice of a whole city?... And a city is larger than a single man?... Perhaps, then, there is more justice in the larger thing, and it will be easier to learn what it is. So, if you're willing, let's first find out what sort of thing justice is in a city and afterwards look for it in the individual, observing the ways in which the smaller is similar to the larger.[9]

This is more than just a clever transition. It points to one of the most elegant features of Plato's *Republic*: the way in which the well-ordered state, ruled by the wise, protected by the courageous, and supplied by temperate and non-envious workers, mirrors the well-ordered psyche, in which emotions and desires are subservient to a rational intellect. One need not ascribe to Plato's anti-democratic, paternalist political theory or even his reason-centered idea of human psychology to appreciate the way in which these two kinds of justice inform one another.

Unjust societies have a tendency to produce psychologically disordered, morally bankrupt individuals (or, put differently, make it circumstantially difficult to adhere to moral ideals). Further, unjust individuals, when sufficiently empowered, can infuse systems and institutions with their wicked intentions. Conversely, just societies are designed to facilitate human development and flourishing, minimizing (as far as possible) psychological disorder and moral corruption and addressing them fairly and humanely where they persist. And just as wicked individuals contribute to unjust systems, virtuous individuals contribute to the creation and maintenance of just systems and institutions.

Thus, Plato posits, in the political sphere, something like what cultural psychologists call "mutual constitution," where individuals influence their society and culture, just as social and cultural institutions simultaneously shape individuals. One could select any number of examples to illustrate this phenomenon: mass incarceration's effect on family structure and thus child development; the fact that contemporary capitalist societies exhibit sky-high rates of depression and anxiety; and the way in which parenting styles accurately predict predispositions to authoritarian governance. But let us think about an example that connects most readily to the overarching theme of this book. Let us think about the issue of systemic or institutional racism and its relation to individual racial prejudice.

We have already seen that liberal anti-racism emphasizes a particular relationship between individual racial prejudice and institutional racial injustice, where the former is generally presumed to be the cause of the latter. I claimed that this sort of view fails to appreciate the extent to which racial prejudice can be the effect of racial injustice as much as its cause. Let us further examine this claim, in the context of the timely issue of racism in policing. A liberal understanding of this issue is likely to assume that it has mostly to do with the prejudices of individual officers and whether those prejudices give rise to discriminatory policies and practices, objectionable uses of force, and so on. Such an understanding lends itself to liberal interventions aiming to reduce prejudice and bias: implicit bias training, cultural competency programs, improved screening and hiring practices, and so on. Such measures might find some success in blocking or rooting out proverbial "bad apples," but they are unlikely to address the deep, systemic racial injustices – internal and external to policing – which give rise to the most pressing injustices in this domain. Further, they fail to consider that the biases they target might not be pre-existing but might themselves be the effect of working in an occupation shaped by these deep structural injustices.

Let us begin with a simple illustration to appreciate this point. Imagine an individual white officer, harboring no racial prejudice but also having had little contact with persons of color outside of his predominately white hometown. Recruited to a large, racially diverse city, let us imagine that he is assigned to patrol a largely Black, economically distressed, high-crime neighborhood. Over a period of years in which the officer's primary interactions with Black individuals take the form of tense, high-stress, high-risk interactions, it is not hard to imagine that this officer might develop negative perceptions of Black communities and individuals – that is, racial prejudice. When we further consider the paramilitary tactics and "warrior mentality" training protocols typical of modern policing, it becomes difficult to see how officers could *not* begin to dehumanize the communities they police, perceiving them as enemy combatants rather than fellow citizens. None of this is intended to excuse the abuses of individual officers or departments, nor to deny that racial prejudice among officers is a serious problem. It is meant only to illustrate that the liberal view, which traces institutional racism to individual prejudice, is ill equipped to understand the complex dynamics of racial injustice in policing.

One might think that the liberal view fares better as a historical explanation for institutional racism. After all, the existence of Black ghettos, paramilitary policing tactics, and the other factors shaping the hypothetical case just described could probably be traced back to the individual prejudices of white law and policy-makers, even if the individual officer's prejudice is best understood as an effect rather than a cause of these factors. But there are also historical illustrations of the reverse kind of causality. I have already discussed the way in which the "intermediate stratum" of whiteness served to integrate disfavored European groups in ways that upheld white supremacy. The concrete role of policing in this process is rarely appreciated, however. In cities where large numbers of Irish immigrants settled, for example, the path to becoming white frequently went through police, fire, and other forms of municipal employment. In the nascent police forces in particular, the "psychological wage" of whiteness took a tangible form: the authority to exercise a "petty sovereignty" over Black Americans and others lower on the racial ladder.[10] This is not to say that Irish Americans or other European groups were wholly free of racial prejudice prior to their arrival in the United States. But it seems unlikely that the pre-existing racism of immigrants was the primary driver of systemic injustices in early American policing. Rather, like the hypothetical officer above, it seems more likely that the adoption of anti-Black racism was an effect (perhaps even the desired effect) of the integration of European immigrants into the U.S. racial regime.

We should not forget that social institutions are, in fact, human creations, not features of a natural landscape or products of divine intervention. Since it is individual and collective human action that shapes these institutions, it is not a mistake to seek moral accountability for social injustice. But this does not mean that moral transformation is necessarily the path to social change. Just as institutional racism can give rise to individual prejudice, so social change can give rise to significant shifts in moral opinion.

Twentieth-century movements for racial justice illustrate this principle. It's not at all obvious that the judicial and legislative victories of the civil rights movement proceeded from a significant shift in white opinion. While it is true that a significant number of white Americans claimed to support, for example, the 1954 *Brown v. Board of Education* decision in its immediate wake, it is also the case that the most significant shift in white opinion occurred in the decades *after* the decision, leading a 1967 National Opinion Research Study to conclude that "by virtue of the ensuing publicity and the expected far-reaching effects on major population groups," the decision "could be anticipated to have had a direct effect on public opinion."[11]

White Americans were even less supportive of the tactics of the movement. A majority of whites claimed in a 1961 Gallup poll that sit-ins, freedom buses, and other tactics of nonviolent civil disobedience were more likely to hurt the movement for racial equality than help it.[12] Of course, these nonviolent methods are now celebrated in the public mythology of the civil rights era, and whites are far less likely to disapprove of them or of the goals of integration and legal equality (in principle if not in practice). Here, too, the timing suggests that shifts in white opinion were a by-product of social change rather than its precondition. The core victories of the movement were the result of the focused, strategic efforts of a small group of lawyers, activists, and organizers, and moral persuasion was just one aspect of a broader political strategy.

The movement for gay rights provides a second, in some ways even more compelling example. As recently as 2006, a majority of Americans opposed same-sex marriage and also reported believing that gay and lesbian relationships were morally wrong. Over the subsequent fifteen years, public opinion changed dramatically, with support for same-sex marriage roughly doubling, and belief in the immorality of same-sex relationships declining by half.[13] Given the timing of the 2015 *Obergefell v. Hodges* decision legalizing same-sex marriage, it might be tempting to assume that this legal victory was driven by the historical shift in public opinion. But this is simplistic and ignores decades of queer activism, which was rarely focused simply on moral persuasion or acceptance. The work of increasing the visibility of gay and lesbian persons in popular culture is often cited as a critical factor in shifting opinion and policy, though it's not obvious that such a politics of representation is equivalent to moral persuasion, even if that seems to have been its result.

What do these examples tell us about the relationship between morality and social change? Again, they call into question the simplistic liberal view that the path to social change begins with moral persuasion, particularly of those who harbor prejudice against or negative perceptions of oppressed and marginalized groups. If moral shifts are as likely to be an effect of institutional change as a cause, the best strategy would be to work simultaneously to change policy and change public opinion, recognizing that in some cases, pursuing the former might be the most effective path to the latter.

This point has more to do with political strategy, perhaps, than moral philosophy. Still, some moral theories do a better job than others of capturing the relationship between institutional justice and the moral/ethical capacities of individuals. As we have seen, modern moral philosophies like Kant's offer decision procedures focused on determining the rightness of actions. The political application of such approaches usually takes the form of a set of rights – moral claims to be treated in certain ways (or not to be mistreated in certain ways) – that eventually come to form the backbone of liberal constitutional states. States of this sort tend to take a minimalist view of justice, prioritizing "the right" over "the good" and aiming to create a state apparatus that leaves individuals with the freedom to decide moral questions on their own.

As we have seen in previous chapters, this sort of liberalism, while often providing a constitutional basis for claims of legal equality, faces significant limits in its ability to address systemic racial injustice. Its minimalist conception of justice and its emphasis on purely legal equality can fail to reach racial injustice where it remains deeply embedded: in economic systems, in culture, and in other extra-legal social institutions. For this reason, it is worth a brief examination of another way of conceiving the relationship between justice and individual morality. Inspired by ancient thinkers as well as those, like Hume, who emphasize the affective character of moral reflection, contemporary virtue ethicists paint a different picture of this relationship, which I will now examine in some detail.

* * *

Without doubt, the most influential philosophical theory of justice in the world of contemporary academic philosophy is that of American philosopher John Rawls. Deeply influenced by Kant, Rawls' political philosophy exemplifies the above description of liberal constitutionalism. Using a thought experiment inspired by the social contract tradition, Rawls asks what basic principles of justice might be agreeable to all if we were to imagine ourselves in an "original position" without knowledge of key features of our lives: our race, gender, socioeconomic status, abilities, and so on. His answer to this question provides the core of his theory of "justice as fairness." At the most basic level, he argues, all persons would want to live in a society that identifies and protects the broadest possible set of individual rights. Such rights would be enjoyed equally by all members of the society. As for social inequalities, Rawls argues that we would want them to meet two key criteria: they would have to be subject to fair equality of opportunity, such that anyone in society would have a meaningful chance of securing the advantages associated with highly compensated or highly esteemed positions, and the inequalities themselves would have to be socially advantageous or, more precisely, be to the "greatest advantage of the least well off" (the so-called Difference Principle).[14]

These principles of justice, once embedded in constitutions and other aspects of the "basic structure" of society, form the basis of what Rawls calls "political liberalism," a vision of society in which the basic rules are agreeable, on purely rational grounds, to a wide variety of groups that hold fundamentally different worldviews and "conceptions of the good." The basic principles of justice, Rawls argues, must be conceived as the subject of an "overlapping consensus" among these groups, and thus the state must be conceived as neutral among them and not dependent for justification on any comprehensive ethical worldview. Thus, Rawls' political liberalism comes to endorse liberal neutrality, seeing justice as the basic organizing principle for societies that feature a wide variety of moral, religious, and other worldviews.[15]

There has been a great deal of debate about how broad such an overlapping consensus can be (a version of the question of how far liberal tolerance should extend) as well as whether a Rawlsian theory of justice can provide a sufficient foundation for Black liberation and other anti-racist projects.[16] Without delving deeply into this debate, I mean only to point out here that Rawls' vision of political liberalism, while grounded in general principles that are certainly relevant to discussions of racial equality and oppression, is not well equipped to capture the dynamics by which social institutions shape individuals. Indeed, it is designed precisely to forestall any such dynamic, insofar as it might be indicative of an allegedly neutral basic structure exerting a substantive moral influence on citizens. Yet a theory that neglects this path of influence risks failing to fully grasp the complex interplay between social justice and individual moral capacities, at least in societies remotely resembling our own. To better appreciate this mutual influence, we should explore the political implications of contemporary virtue ethics.

New Zealand philosopher Rosalind Hursthouse provides one promising path here. In a brief but powerful essay entitled "After Hume's Justice," Hursthouse argues against liberal political theories that proceed by identifying certain "natural," pre-political rights (allegedly including property rights) and then conceiving of social justice instrumentally, as the means for enshrining and protecting those rights. As an alternative, she proposes that we invert this order, arguing that

> "the logically prior concept is that of a properly functioning society; justice is then specified as the virtue or excellence of such a society, and the laws of justice as those which are in place in such a society; and rights come last, as those things which such laws establish as mine and thine (and ours and theirs.)"[17]

To specify what a "properly functioning society" entails, Hursthouse draws upon the Aristotelian idea of *eudaemonia*, often translated as 'happiness' but meaning something more like 'human flourishing.' A properly functioning society, then, is one that contributes to the human flourishing (or, in perhaps more familiar terms, the healthy development) of its members.

This represents in some ways a more exacting standard of social justice than the minimalist conceptions of Rawls and other liberals. It is grounded in a conception of what human beings are like and what basic human needs societies should strive to meet. But such an account need not be oppressively homogenous. Just as Rawls' basic principles might be the subject of overlapping consensus, so too a conception of human flourishing could be informed by a wide variety of inputs, from the best available biological and psychological science to the cultural, moral, and religious views of a wide variety of the world's peoples.

This sort of approach, and its capacity to embrace pluralism, is illustrated by another influential virtue ethicist, American philosopher Martha Nussbaum. Nussbaum, along with Indian economist Amartya Sen and others, developed the "capabilities approach" to human development, an approach with both philosophical and practical import. Also drawing from Aristotelian virtue ethics, Nussbaum argues that the best way of measuring individual and societal well-being is not via quantitative measures like gross domestic product, nor even the liberal benchmarks of human and civil rights. Rather, she suggests that well-being is best measured by the standard of human capabilities: what actual human beings are able to do and to be in their lives. Unlike Sen, who develops his capability approach as a theory of freedom, Nussbaum develops an actual list of central capabilities, which refer to bodily health and integrity, intellectual and emotional life, control over the material and political conditions of one's existence, "practical reason" (the ability to "form a conception of the good and critically reflect on it"), and more.[18] Thus, her list includes a wide variety of specific metrics, which might be actualized in a wide variety of ways in different cultural, national, and social contexts.

Like Hursthouse, Nussbaum does not rely on causal claims about whether moral transformation drives social change or vice versa, but it does assert a logical priority of the ethical, in the sense that whether or not a society is just or "well-ordered" depends upon its ability to "produce" morally capable, socially responsible, generally thriving persons and communities (an "ethical" vision in the broad sense in which virtue ethics employs the term). Further, her inclusion of "practical reason" in her list of central human capabilities illustrates that the ability to develop the sorts of moral sensitivity and responsiveness required to, for example, reflect upon how systemic racial inequality has impacted one's life experience, is significantly shaped by social and institutional forces. Thus, it captures not only the ability of moral discourse to drive social and institutional change but also the ability of social and institutional forces to enable or constrain moral life.

What does all of this mean for the analysis of privilege politics, interest convergence, and anti-racism generally? For one, it means that (as I have now said repeatedly) an approach that focuses primarily on moral persuasion and psychological transformation, without paying sufficient attention to institutional context and the psychological biases that impede such efforts, is not likely to be an effective path to social transformation. If we truly want to address racial inequality and injustice, we must attend to the institutions that feed it. While the original analyses of the "wages of whiteness" and "white skin privilege" did just this, connecting a system of racial privilege to the imperatives of an evolving, post-emancipation form of racial capitalism, the deradicalized, class-blind forms of privilege politics prevalent today have largely concealed this connection, replacing it with a form of moral instruction that neglects concrete interests with the potential to forge powerful interracial alliances for racial and economic justice. The virtue ethical approaches described above encourage us to move beyond liberal strategies of bias reduction and narrowly legal efforts to sustain formal racial equality, and to embrace broad, imaginative visions of what an anti-racist society might look like. If we then work to change institutions to reflect this vision, appealing to the self and collective interests of white Americans and Americans of color alike, white moral transformation may well be an organic by-product of such a process. A strategy such as this has the potential to activate a virtuous kind of circularity, where structural change shapes individual attitudes and beliefs in ways that make possible further structural change. Such a description may sound exceedingly idealistic when stated in this general form. But when pursued in specific domains, guiding concrete racial justice projects, glimpses of such a vision become increasingly visible, and its general viability becomes correspondingly less implausible.

Given the central role of colleges and universities in disseminating the idea of white privilege and its corresponding politics, not to mention my own familiarity with these institutions, it seems appropriate to conclude the book with an analysis of how the politics of privilege connects with the institutional imperatives of contemporary higher education and how an interest convergence approach might reshape the efforts of educational institutions.

Notes

1 Immanuel Kant, *Grounding for the Metaphysics of Morals: On a Supposed Right to Lie because of Philanthropic Concerns*. 3rd ed. Trans. James E. Ellington. (Indianapolis: Hackett Publishing, 1993): 16.
2 See David Livingston Smith, *The Most Dangerous Animal: Human Nature and the Origins of War* (New York: St. Martin's Press, 2007) and David Livingstone Smith, *Less Than Human: Why We Demean, Enslave, and Exterminate Others* (New York: St. Martin's Press, 2011).
3 Charles Mills. *The Racial Contract* (Ithaca: Cornell University Press, 1999): 27.
4 Kant, *Grounding for the Metaphysics of Morals*, 10.
5 Charles Mills, "'Heart' Attack: A Critique of Jorge Garcia's Volitional Conception of Racism," *Journal of Ethics* 7 (2003): 40.

6 See David Brookman, and Joshua Kalla, "Durably Reducing Transphobia: A Field Experiment on Door-to-Door Canvassing," *Science* 352.6282 (2016): 220-224.

7 L. Santos, J. Voelkel, R. Willer, and J. Zaki, "Belief in the Utility of Cross-Partisan Empathy Reduces Partisan Animosity and Facilitates Persuasion," *Psychological Science* 33.9 (2022): 1557–1573.

8 Here, I use the terms 'morality' and 'ethics' interchangeably, in ways that would probably give moral philosophers pause. While there are important technical distinctions one might make between these two forms of normative inquiry, none strike me as particularly helpful in the context of this discussion.

9 Plato, *Republic*. Trans. G.M.A. Grube. (Indianapolis: Hackett, 1992): 43.

10 See Ben Brucato, "Fabricating the Color Line in a White Democracy: From Slave Catchers to Petty Sovereigns," *Theoria: A Journal of Social and Political Theory* 61.141 (2014): 30–54.

11 Mildred A. Schwartz, *Trends in White Attitudes Toward Negroes* (Chicago: University of Chicago National Opinion Research Center, 1967): 35.

12 R.J. Reinhart, "Protests Seen as Harming the Civil Rights Movement in the 1960s." *Gallop*. May, 1961.

13 See Gallup, *LGBT Rights*. Retrieved April 20, 2023, from https://news.gallup.com/poll/1651/gay-lesbian-rights.aspx.

14 John Rawls, *A Theory of Justice* (Cambridge: Harvard University Press, 1999).

15 John Rawls, *Political Liberalism* (New York: Colombia University Press, 2005).

16 For the latter debate, see Charles Mills, "Rawls on Race/Race in Rawls," *The Southern Journal of Philosophy* 48 (2009): 161–184; Tommie Shelby, "Race and Social Justice: Rawlsian Considerations," *Fordham Law Review* 72.5 (2004): 1697–1714; Charles Mills, "Retrieving Rawls for Racial Justice? A Critique of Tommie Shelby," *Critical Philosophy of Race* 1.1 (2013): 1–27; Tommie Shelby, "Racial Realities and Corrective Justice: A Reply to Charles Mills," *Critical Philosophy of Race*, 1.2 (2013): 145–162.

17 Rosalind Hursthouse, "After Hume's Justice," *Proceedings of the Aristotelian Society* 91 (1990–1991): 235.

18 Martha Nussbaum, *Women and Human Development: The Capabilities Approach* (Cambridge: Cambridge University Press, 2001).

CONCLUSION

Re-centering Racial Justice

In the previous chapter, I explored the relationship between the moral capacities of individuals and the driving imperatives of institutions in some detail, emphasizing the ways in which the latter can shape the former. It is only fitting, then, that I conclude with some reflections on the institutional context with which I am most familiar, that of the contemporary American university. It is fitting not just because of my own experience, of course, but also because, as we have seen, colleges and universities have been at the center of the process by which the idea of white privilege has been captured, deradicalized, and popularized. For reasons that I will shortly detail, this process is also bound up with the development of Diversity, Equity, and Inclusion (DEI) initiatives within higher education, which arose in large part to adapt to legal challenges to the justice-based interventions of universities. To understand this historical context, let me begin with the landmark affirmative action case *Regents of the University of California v. Bakke*.

In 1974, in the still rippling wake of the civil rights advances of the 1960s, a white 34-year-old named Alan Bakke applied to the University of California Davis' medical school for the second year in a row. His first application, submitted late in the cycle, was narrowly rejected, and administrators had encouraged him to apply again. After being rejected a second time, Bakke sued, arguing that the school's two-tiered admissions scheme, with a regular admissions category and a special admissions category for self-identified "disadvantaged" candidates, violated his Fourteenth Amendment right to "equal protection of the laws."

The case, often viewed as a vindication of affirmative action in higher education, produced no fewer than six separate opinions among the nine justices. The legally binding plurality opinion, authored by Justice Lewis

DOI: 10.4324/9781003461210-8

Powell, found in favor of Bakke, ordering his admission to the medical school. Powell reasoned that the separate admissions categories essentially barred Bakke from consideration in the "special" category, in virtue of his race, and thus violated the Equal Protection Clause. More broadly, then, the decision prohibited quota-like admissions policies, in which a certain number of seats are set aside for racially disadvantaged candidates. However, the decision also upheld the constitutionality of race-conscious affirmative action policies, provided that they considered the race of applicants holistically, as one factor among others, in a single, undivided competition.

It was not merely the form of UC Davis' race-conscious admissions policy that garnered the Court's ire, however, but its content as well. Like many affirmative action programs of the time, UC Davis' special admissions program was designed explicitly to address racial injustice. Its goals, as summarized in Powell's decision, included "reducing the historic deficit of traditionally disfavored minorities in medical schools and in the medical profession; countering the effects of societal discrimination [and] increasing the number of physicians who will practice in communities currently underserved." In addition to these justice-based goals, UC Davis included a fourth, specifically pedagogical aim: "obtaining the educational benefits that flow from an ethnically diverse student body."[1]

The three justice-based goals were viewed with significant skepticism by the Court. Of the UC system whose admissions program was under scrutiny, Powell wrote "its broad mission is education, not the formulation of any legislative policy or the adjudication of particular claims of illegality."[2] Expressing a pallid half-sympathy with concerns about addressing racial injustice, Powell nonetheless declared colleges and universities "not competent to make those decisions." Seeking a "compelling state interest" in the use of race to such ends, the Court found none. Only the diversity-based goal survived the Court's strict scrutiny, with Powell declaring the cultivation of a racially and otherwise diverse student body a "clearly permissible goal for an institution of higher education."[3]

While UC's arguments demonstrate that concerns about diversity surely predate the *Bakke* decision, it is fair to say that that decision, by severely restricting justice-based rationales for affirmative action, effected something like a "diversity turn" in university admissions policy. Any school that sought to retain a race-conscious admissions policy would now have to frame that policy in terms of the general value of diversity (which, notably, extends to white students as well as students of color). Institutions that presumably cared about racial justice dutifully adapted in order to continue their mission in ways that were legally secure.

Whether or not this shift was initially strategic, in the nearly half-century since the case was decided, institutional approaches to racial progress have fully embraced the diversity framework encouraged by *Bakke*. Beyond diversifying admissions, the diversity approach has been extended to faculty development and hiring, curricular reform, student life, and more. Increasingly, these efforts are coordinated by dedicated administrative units staffed by DEI professionals. In many ways, this is a positive development, increasing access to the enrichment and social mobility pathways that higher education provides and challenging the Eurocentricity and white supremacy embedded in so many academic pursuits. Indeed, in the preceding chapters, I have described the benefits that flow from diverse educational settings as one of the key advantages that an interest convergence approach can bring to movements for educational justice.

But the rise of DEI administrative bureaucracies in higher education also reflects the process of "elite capture" described in the first chapter. Gradually divorced from disciplinary knowledge, DEI enterprises have filled the resulting void with the deradicalized, pseudo-therapeutic framework of privilege politics. Just as privilege politics substitutes white self-reflection for social transformation in the broader public sphere, so within the university it becomes less about challenging entrenched forms of power and domination (both internally and externally) and more about disciplining its academic workforce, enforcing adherence to superficially progressive ideologies and ensuring that the educational "product" on offer is widely appealing and unlikely to alienate its student "consumers."

My point here is not that institutionalized DEI work is inappropriate or unnecessary but rather that it is insufficient, and increasingly ineffective, insofar as achieving real diversity, equity, or inclusion would require colleges and universities to reclaim their role as agents of justice and social transformation. Consider that, in roughly the same period that the visibility and stature of DEI work have increased, state-level support for higher education has dramatically decreased, shifting a greater percentage of costs onto students, through steadily increasing tuition. This has made higher education less accessible to a wide swath of the population and saddled those who do manage to access it with a level of debt that significantly reduces its economic advantages. Further, while racial inequalities in access surely persist, they have gradually declined over a period of decades, while income-based inequalities have gradually increased.[4] This creates an ideal environment for a racially diverse elite to translate educational access into class advantage. Once empowered, such an elite is more likely to focus on securing conditions favorable to their ascension within the institutions they help to manage, rather than work to increase access to those institutions in ways that might radically transform them. Their inward-looking approach to the culture and curriculum of their institutions mirrors (and frequently relies upon) the inward-looking methods of the politics of privilege and is unlikely to bring about significant structural change for many of the same reasons.

These factors loom especially large in the wake of the *Students for Fair Admissions* (SFFA) decisions, which essentially overturned even the weaker, diversity-centering precedent set by *Bakke* and the more recent *Grutter v. Bollinger* case, virtually prohibiting the use of race as a factor in college admissions decisions. While such a ruling is unfortunate, illustrating the racially regressive priorities of an increasingly radical and out-of-step Court, it has also resulted in a wave of important analyses of how to ensure and expand college access in the post-SFFA era. Many of these analyses have noted that affirmative action policies disproportionately affect a small number of highly selective institutions and are essentially irrelevant to the large number of less selective institutions that most students of color attend.[5] As a result, expanding access to and affordability of these non-elite institutions could be a welcome by-product of the abolition of race-based affirmative action. Similarly, many institutions have stressed the importance of sustaining racial diversity through socio-economic factors like income, geography, first-generation student status, and more. Both of these strategies have the potential to lift up working-class white students as well as students of color, making the post-SFFA era ripe for articulating converging interests around educational access.

But, one might object, what more can colleges and universities do beyond ensuring that they are as internally inclusive, welcoming, and diverse as possible within the constraints imposed by the society in which they are embedded? Higher education has little control, one might argue, over increasing economic inequality, deindustrialization, declining state funding, and other factors that have reduced access to its social advantages. What's wrong, then, with ensuring that one's own institution functions in ways that are at least internally just?

This sort of objection underestimates the extent to which higher education is complicit in each of the developments just mentioned and the central functional role of colleges and universities in an information-centric advanced capitalism. In countries where higher education is the main path to economic advancement, colleges and universities simply are economic institutions, even if they are not *only* economic institutions. This means that whatever criticisms one might deploy against the radically unequal, exploitative, marginalizing, and colonial economies that structure the modern world will have serious implications for institutions of higher education. This, in turn, entails that higher education is to some degree accountable for these injustices, in ways that demand some response.

What, then, is the appropriate response? How do colleges and universities reclaim their role as change-makers and agents of justice, beyond diversification efforts that often fail to deliver justice beyond the university gates? In what follows, I will briefly outline a proposal for justice-centered university work, work that breaks down barriers between "town" and "gown" and aims to address trenchant forms of social injustice through a restorative lens. I also show how this proposal builds upon the interest convergence approach I have defended in these pages.

* * *

I began this book with a description of a pedagogical exercise typical of privilege-based approaches to anti-racism. I will end it with a description of a pedagogical project that reflects the interest convergence approach that I have defended as an alternative to the ineffective politics and pedagogy of privilege. Variously referred to as "service-learning," "community-engaged learning," and "experiential learning," efforts to bring students out of the classroom and into the broader community have become more common in recent decades, canonized as one of the "high-impact practices" that effective instructors and institutions employ.[6] These programs have not always been guided by robust visions of social justice. Traditional service-learning practices have often focused disproportionately (sometimes exclusively) on the benefits of community-engaged learning practices for students and neglected the benefits to community partners and to the community more broadly. The result is an inegalitarian and paternalistic form of community engagement, in which universities decide whom and how to help, and the community is viewed as a passive recipient of its noblesse oblige. Programs conceived in this way often exacerbate racial and economic tensions, sending disproportionately white, relatively advantaged students into economically distressed communities of color, typically with little understanding of the issues these communities face.

Scholars and practitioners of community-engaged learning have increasingly begun to challenge these colonial forms of engagement, however, often under the conceptual umbrella of "critical service-learning." In a seminal article, Tania Mitchell outlines the differences between "traditional" and "critical" service-learning.[7] In the first place, critical service-learning is oriented to social change. This means that, while it may, like traditional forms of service-learning, strive to meet specific community needs, it does so with an eye toward the way in which those needs arise from structural injustices and therefore works to eliminate the structural injustices as well as meet the needs. Second, critical service-learning strives to redistribute power, challenging unequal relationships, for example, between well-resourced universities and under-resourced community partners, between professors and community practitioners, or between students and the community members with whom they work. Relatedly, critical service-learning strives to develop authentic relationships with community partners, relationships that entail mutual respect and mutual benefit and that evolve constructively over time.

Framed in this way, community-engaged learning efforts avoid extractive relationships, where the community is viewed as a resource for student development but not a genuine partner. Interestingly, Mitchell warns also of diversity-based approaches that frame community engagement in terms of "encountering difference." "Too often," she claims, "the 'difference' experienced in the service setting is reduced to issues of diversity. This action serves to essentialize and reinforce the dichotomies of 'us' and 'them,' reproducing the hierarchies critical service-learning seeks to undo."[8] By focusing on transforming power relations and pursuing social change, Mitchell makes clear the ways in which critical service-learning moves beyond the standard diversity framework described above.

Mitchell does not explicitly present critical service-learning as an anti-racist project, but it is certainly more conducive to anti-racism than its "traditional" counterpart. This compels us to ask: how does critical service-learning relate to the competing approaches to anti-racism described in this book, the politics of privilege, and the interest convergence approach? Perhaps obviously, developing authentic relationships based on shared and mutually beneficial goals requires something very much like an interest convergence approach, where community partners and university personnel seek areas of overlap between their interests and desired outcomes. Further, if my arguments in the previous chapters are correct, an approach seeking social transformation is better aligned with the interest convergence approach than with privilege-based approaches.

Given the emphasis on transforming power relations, one might think that reflection on racial privilege and other kinds of inequality would be crucial to achieving a more egalitarian distribution of power. Mitchell acknowledges as much, saying that "students engaged in service-learning will undoubtedly have greater social privilege than those whom they encounter at their service placements"[9]. She describes this kind of privilege as including inequalities based on "race, class, age, ability, or education level," among other factors, and insists that critical service-learning participants remain aware of and reflective about the power differentials these inequalities can produce. But she also warns against becoming engrossed in these power differentials to a degree that we fail to address the unjust structures that produce them. Privilege politics, with its introspective attunement to white moral improvement, has been shown in these pages to make just this mistake. Especially in situations where race- and class-based privileges are distributed unevenly across collaborating groups, an approach taking privilege recognition and white psychological transformation as its primary goals is unlikely to create the conditions for authentic and productive collaboration. Rather, privilege-based approaches are likely to produce an extractive model of community engagement, where the community setting is viewed primarily as a laboratory for student self-improvement.

Critical service-learning practices provide a useful illustration of how colleges and universities might move beyond the ineffective liberal anti-racism of privilege politics and begin to employ an interest convergence approach. By working in small but impactful ways to transform injustice in their own backyards, institutions of higher education may begin to break down some of the barriers between "town" and "gown," combat accusations of elitism, and regain some lost trust from groups for whom access to higher education has been precarious. What does this actually look like in practice?

In a city with tragically high levels of childhood lead exposure, a local university forms a "lead innovation team," employing chemists, engineers, social scientists, and their students to develop a cheap, freely distributed home lead-testing kit, working with neighborhood organizations to raise awareness of lead poisoning and its sources, and helping residents access grants for lead abatement.[10]

A sociology professor offers a course on "social action," which is centered on student-driven campaigns for change, many of which partner with local organizers and community partners and win impressive victories like an increase in the local minimum wage.[11]

An interdisciplinary justice studies program develops a course exploring affordable housing, and its students work with a group of community members to secure a grant for a multi-family housing cooperative the group is developing in a disinvested, historically Black neighborhood.[12]

These initiatives and others like them make small but measurable progress on issues of racial and economic justice, as they simultaneously teach students skills and strategies for pursuing real change. Though currently not a central focus of academic activity outside of smaller, teaching-focused institutions, critical service-learning projects like these have the potential to re-center justice in the work of colleges and universities and rebuild trust among communities whose access to higher education has been precarious.

We should not be naïve about the viability of a justice-centered project like this. Critical service-learning projects are often less structured and require a greater measure of flexibility than traditional forms of service-learning. No doubt, it is easier for instructors to coordinate with an established homeless shelter or soup kitchen than to work alongside a nascent group of organizers aiming to resist the destruction of affordable housing units to make way for city-subsidized luxury housing. University administrators, who are often more eager to forge partnerships with corporate interests and employers than community change agents, may push back against such initiatives with concerns about legal liability, political partisanship, and mission alignment or in even more direct ways. But a critical mass of faculty and staff, with allies in the community prepared to hold schools accountable for their rhetoric of good citizenship and concern, may be able to push such initiatives forward even against the resistance of unsympathetic administrators.

The success that the academic purveyors of the politics of privilege have had in disseminating its rituals and rhetoric in the public sphere should remind us of the significant power of institutions of higher education. A less corporate-friendly, more radical form of anti-racism will surely face obstacles that the deradicalized liberal politics of privilege has not. Still, there is reason for cautious optimism. The formally educated are inclined to chuckle self-assuredly at punchlines about the increasing stupidity of the uneducated masses. Meanwhile, those masses are thirstier than ever for ideas, critical perspectives, and new ways of organizing the world. Privilege-based academic anti-racism has had little to offer them, beyond shame-inducing narratives of complicity and victimization. The resulting lacuna has been filled by a motley crew of conspiracy theorists, pseudo-intellectuals, and outright fascists.

Racial inequality is, of course, very real, and we should resist political narratives that aim to deny it, control our awareness of it, or punish those who would draw attention to it, as an increasingly emboldened group of racist policymakers are now aiming to do. Economic inequality is also real and increasingly stark. It overlaps significantly with racial inequality, given the lasting economic impacts of racial oppression. But the overlap is not total, and we should resist approaches that aim to reduce economic disadvantage to racial disadvantage, or ignore the former in favor of the latter, as I have argued that the class-blind politics of privilege does. Instead, anti-racist academics should find ways to speak to the diverse groups that have been left behind by a post-industrial form of capitalism that higher education has too often served unquestioningly.

Critical service-learning is one path to this sort of engagement, but it cannot be the only one. Academics and academic institutions must work diligently to regain their place as one of the primary institutions guiding our society through a period of inevitable social transformation. Moving closer to a future of genuine racial and economic justice, and away from the increasingly dystopian future that global racial capitalism is accelerating toward, requires a more powerful critical framework than the navel-gazing politics of privilege. Anti-racist academics must lend our intellectual efforts and resources to this task by helping to articulate interests that can draw together diverse groups, forging powerful alliances for justice. The interest convergence approach I have offered as an alternative to the politics of privilege aims to provide a theoretical foundation for this work and to help to clear away some dust on a new path toward racial and economic justice. I offer it with the utmost respect to the scholars, organizers, and activists who have inspired it and with a cautious but impatient hope for the alternative future that it may help to reveal.

Notes

1 Regents of Univ. of California v. Bakke, 438 U.S. 265 (1978): 306.
2 Ibid, 309.
3 Ibid, 311–12.
4 See Greg Duncan, and Richard Murnane, "Growing Income Inequality Threatens American Education," *Phi Delta Kappan* 95 (2014), 8–14. See also G.J. Duncan, and R.J. Murnane, eds. *Whither Opportunity? Rising Inequality, Schools, and Children's Life Chances* (New York, NY: Russell Sage Foundation & Spencer Foundation, 2011).
5 While this is true of race-based admissions policies specifically, the SFFA decisions set a dangerous precedent that could be extended to other, much more impactful contexts, for example scholarships and forms of financial aid and that target students of color. It remains to be seen whether the emboldened forces of white supremacy will aim to build upon the precedent in this way.
6 See George D. Kuh, *High-Impact Educational Practices: What They Are, Who Has Access to Them, and Why They Matter* (Washington D.C.: American Association of Colleges and Universities, 2008)
7 Tania D. Mitchell, "Traditional vs. Critical Service-Learning: Engaging the Literature to Differentiate Two Models," *Michigan Journal of Community Service Learning* 14.2 (2008): 50–65.
8 Ibid, 56.
9 Ibid.
10 See M. Tighe et al., "Validation of a Screening Kit to Identify Environmental Lead Hazards," *Environmental Research* 181 (2020): 108892, which relates to the work of the Notre Dame Lead Innovation Team (ND LIT).
11 See San Jose State University professor Scott Myers-Lipton's book *Change! A Guide to Teaching Social Action* (New York: Routledge, 2022), which expands upon the model Myers-Lipton employs in the course.
12 This is my own course and program, developed here at Saint Mary's College in South Bend, Indiana.

BIBLIOGRAPHY

Alba, Richard. *The Great Demographic Illusion: Majority, Minority, and the Expanding American Mainstream* (Princeton, NJ: Princeton University Press, 2020).

Allen, Theodore. *The Invention of the White Race. Vol. I. Racial Oppression and Social Control* (London: Verso, 1994).

Ballew M. et al. *Which Racial/Ethnic Groups Care Most About Climate Change?* (New Haven, CT: Yale Program on Climate Change Communication, 2020).

Bell, Derrick A. "Brown v. Board of Education and the Interest Convergence Dilemma," *Harvard Law Review* 93.3 (1980): 518–533.

Benegal, Salil D. "The Spillover of Race and Racial Attitudes into Public Opinion about Climate Change," *Environmental Politics* 27.4 (2018): 733–756.

Bhattacharrya, Gargi. *Rethinking Racial Capitalism: Questions of Reproduction and Survival* (New York: Rowman and Littlefield, 2018).

Brookman, David, and Joshua Kalla. "Durably Reducing Transphobia: A Field Experiment on Door-to-Door Canvassing," *Science* 352.6282 (2016): 220–224.

Brucato, Ben. "Fabricating the Color Line in a White Democracy: From Slave Catchers to Petty Sovereigns." *Theoria: A Journal of Social and Political Theory* 61.141 (2014): 30–54.

Case, Ann, and Angus Deaton. *Deaths of Despair and the Future of Capitalism* (Princeton: Princeton University Press, 2021).

Chaikin, A.L., and J.M. Darley. "Victim or Perpetrator? Defensive Attribution of Responsibility and the Need for Order and Justice," *Journal of Personality and Social Psychology* 25.2 (1973): 268–275.

Clay, Phillip, and Timothy Pattison. "The Process of Neighborhood Upgrading and Gentrification" (Master's Thesis, Massachusetts Institute of Technology, 1977).

Dewey, John. *Democracy and Education: An Introduction to the Philosophy of Education* (New York: The Free Press, 1944).

Du Bois, W.E.B. *Black Reconstruction in America: An Essay toward a History of the Part Which Black Folk Played in the Attempt to Reconstruct Democracy in America, 1860–1880* (New York: Oxford University Press, 2007).

Duncan, Greg, and R.J. Murnane, eds. *Whither Opportunity? Rising Inequality, Schools, and Children's Life Chances* (New York, NY: Russell Sage Foundation & Spencer Foundation, 2011).

Duncan, Greg, and Richard Murnane. "Growing Income Inequality Threatens American Education," *Phi Delta Kappan* 95 (2014): 8–14.

Dyer, Thomas. *Theodore Roosevelt and the Idea of Race* (Baton Rouge: Louisiana State University Press, 1992).

Edwards, Kirsten T. "This Bridge Called My Body: Talking Race Through Embodying Difference," in *Exploring Race in Predominantly White Classrooms: Scholars of Color Reflect*, ed. George Yancy, and Maria del Guadalupe Davidson (New York: Routledge, 2014).

Emmons, William R., Ana H. Kent, and Lowell R. Ricketts. "The Bigger They Are, The Harder They Fall: The Decline of the White Working Class," *The Demographics of Wealth* 3 (2018).

Fanon, Franz. *The Wretched of the Earth*. Trans. Richard Philcox (New York: Grove Press, 2004).

Fourlas, George. "Being a Target: On the Racialization of Middle Eastern Americans," *Critical Philosophy of Race* 3.1 (2015): 101–123.

Franklin, A. Todd. "A Letter to My Kinfolk on the One Hundred and Fiftieth Anniversary of the Emancipation," in *Exploring Race in Predominantly White Classrooms: Scholars of Color Reflect*, ed. George Yancy and Maria del Guadalupe Davidson (New York: Routledge, 2014).

Franklin, Benjamin. "Observations Concerning the Increase of Mankind and the Peopling of Countries," in *The Autobiography and Other Writings*, ed. Ben Franklin (New York: Oxford University Press, 2008).

Fraser, Nancy. *Cannibal Capitalism: How Our System is Devouring Democracy, Care, and the Planet – And What We Can Do About It* (London: Verso, 2022).

Furnham, A. "Belief in a Just World: Research Progress over the Past Decade," *Personality and Individual Differences* 34 (2003): 795–817.

Gallagher, Charles A. "Miscounting Race: Explaining Misperceptions in Racial Group Size," *Sociological Perspectives* 46.3 (2003): 381–396.

Gilens, Martin. "'Race Coding' and White Opposition to Welfare," *The American Political Science Review* 90.3 (1996): 593–604.

Glass, Kathy. "Race-ing the Curriculum: Reflections on a Pedagogy of Social Change" in *Exploring Race in Predominantly White Classrooms: Scholars of Color Reflect*, ed. George Yancy and Maria del Guadalupe Davidson (New York: Routledge, 2014).

Griffin, Paul, and C. R. Heede, *The Carbon Majors Database: Methodology Report* (London: CDP Worldwide, 2017).

Guinier, Lani. "From Racial Liberalism to Racial Literacy: Brown v. Board of Education and the Interest-Divergence Dilemma," *Journal of American History* 91.1 (2004): 92–118.

Guinier, Lani, and Gerald Torres. *The Miner's Canary: Enlisting Race, Resisting Power, Transforming Democracy* (Cambridge, MA: Harvard University Press, 2003).

Gutierrez, David. "Little School on the Prairie: The Overlooked Plight of Rural Education," *Harvard Political Review*. February 10, 2016.

Hahn, R.A. *Racial and Ethnic Segregation as a Core Social Determinant of Public Health and Health Equity: A Persistent Public Health Challenge in the United States*, Unpublished Manuscript (Atlanta, GA: Center for Disease Control and Prevention, n.d.).

Haider, Asad. *Mistaken Identity: Race and Class in the Age of Trump* (London: Verso, 2018).

Hall, Shannon. "Exxon Knew About Climate Change Almost 40 Years Ago." *Scientific American*. October 26, 2015.

Haney Lopez, Ian. *White By Law: The Legal Construction of Race* (New York: NYU Press, 2006).

Hoffman, Matthew M. "The Illegitimate President: Minority Vote Dilution and the Electoral College," *The Yale Law Journal* 105.4 (January 1996): 935–1021.

Honneth, Axel. *The Struggle for Recognition: The Moral Grammar of Social Conflicts*. Trans. Joel Anderson (Cambridge, MA: MIT Press, 1996).

hooks, bell. *Where We Stand: Class Matters* (London: Routledge, 2000).

Horkheimer, Max, and Theodor Adorno. *The Dialectic of Enlightenment: Philosophical Fragments*. Trans. Edmund Jephcott (Stanford: Stanford University Press, 2007).

Hursthouse, Rosalind. "After Hume's Justice," *Proceedings of the Aristotelian Society* 91 (1990–1991): 229–245.

Ignatiev, Noel. *How the Irish Became White* (New York: Routledge, 1995).

IPCC Summary for Policymakers, in *Climate Change 2022: Impacts, Adaptation and Vulnerability. Contribution of Working Group II to the Sixth Assessment Report of the Intergovernmental Panel on Climate Change* (Cambridge, UK: Cambridge University Press, 2022).

Janoff-Bulman, Ronnie, Christine Timko, and Linda L. Carli. "Cognitive Biases in Blaming the Victim," *Journal of Experimental Social Psychology* 21.2 (1985): 161–177.

Jardina, Ashley. *White Identity Politics* (Cambridge, UK: Cambridge University Press, 2019).

Jost, John T., Banaji R. Mahzarin, and Brian A. Nosek. "A Decade of System Justification Theory: Accumulated Evidence of Conscious and Unconscious Bolstering of the Status Quo," *International Society of Political Psychology* 25.6 (2004): 881–919.

Kant, Immanuel. *Grounding for the Metaphysics of Morals: On a Supposed Right to Lie because of Philanthropic Concerns*. Trans. James E. Ellington. 3rd ed. (Indianapolis, IN: Hackett Publishing, 1993):

Kendall, Frances E. *Understanding White Privilege: Creating Pathways to Authentic Relationships Across Race*. 2nd ed. (New York: Routledge, 2013).

Kimmel, Michael S, and Abby L. Ferber, eds. *Privilege: A Reader*. 3rd ed. (Boulder, CO: Westview Press, 2013).

King, Martin Luther. *Where Do We Go from Here? Chaos or Community?* (Boston: Beacon Press, 2010).

Kohn, Margaret. *The Death and Life of the Urban Commonwealth* (Oxford: Oxford University Press, 2016).

Koshy, Susan, Lisa Marie Cacho, Jodi A. Bryd, and Brian Jordan Jefferson, eds. *Colonial Racial Capitalism* (Durham, NC: Duke University Press, 2022).

Kuh, George D. *High-Impact Educational Practices: What They Are, Who Has Access to Them, and Why They Matter* (Washington, DC: American Association of Colleges and Universities, 2008).

Kymlicka, Will. *Multicultural Citizenship* (Oxford: Oxford University Press, 1995).

Lally, Kevin. *Whiteness and Antiracism: Beyond White Privilege Pedagogy* (New York: Teachers College Press, 2022).

Lerner, Melvin J.. "The Desire for Justice and Reactions to Victims," in *Altruism and Helping Behavior*, ed. J. Macaulay and L. Berkowitz (New York: Academic Press, 1970).

Lerner, Melvin J. *The Belief in a Just World: A Fundamental Delusion* (New York: Plenum Press, 1980).

Lerner, Melvin J., and Dale T. Miller. "Just World Research and the Attribution Process: Looking Back and Ahead" *Psychological Bulletin* 85.5 (1978): 1030–1051.

Lerner, Melvin J., and C.H. Simmons. "Observer's Reaction to the 'Innocent Victim': Compassion or Rejection?" *Journal of Personality and Social Psychology* 4 (1966): 203–210.

MacWilliams, Matthew C. *The Rise of Trump: America's Authoritarian Spring* (Amherst, MA: Amherst University Press, 2016).

Margolin, Leslie. "Unpacking the Invisible Knapsack: The Invention of White Privilege Pedagogy," *Cogent Social Sciences* 1.1 (2015): 1053183.

Marx, Karl. "On the Jewish Question," in *The Marx-Engels Reader*, ed. Robert Tucker (New York: Norton & Company, 1978).

McGhee, Heather. *The Sum of Us: What Racism Costs Everyone and How We Can Prosper Together* (New York: One World Press, 2021).

McIntosh, Peggy. "White Privilege: Unpacking the Invisible Knapsack," *Independent School* 49.2. (1990): 31–35.

Mickelson, Roslyn. "Twenty-first Century Social Science on School Racial Diversity and Educational Outcomes," *Ohio State Law Journal* 69 (2008): 1173.

Mickelson, Roslyn. "School Integration and K-12 Outcomes: An Updated Quick Synthesis of the Social Science Evidence," *The National Coalition on School Diversity*, Brief no. 5 (October 2016).

Mill, John Stuart. *On Liberty* (Kitchener, ON: Batoche Books, 2001).

Miller, J.G. "Culture and the Development of Everyday Social Explanation," *Journal of Personality and Social Psychology* 46.5 (1984): 961–978.

Mills, Charles. *The Racial Contract* (Ithaca, NY: Cornell University Press, 1999).

Mills, Charles. "'Heart' Attack: A Critique of Jorge Garcia's Volitional Conception of Racism," *Journal of Ethics* 7 (2003): 29–62.

Mills, Charles. "Rawls on Race/Race in Rawls," *The Southern Journal of Philosophy* 48 (2009): 161–184.

Mills, Charles. "Retrieving Rawls for Racial Justice? A Critique of Tommie Shelby," *Critical Philosophy of Race* 1.1 (2013): 1–27.

Mitchell, Tania D. "Traditional vs. Critical Service-Learning: Engaging the Literature to Differentiate Two Models," *Michigan Journal of Community Service Learning* 14.2 (2008): 50–65.

Monahan, Michael. "The Concept of Privilege: A Critical Appraisal," *South African Journal of Philosophy* 33.1 (2014): 73–83.

Moskowitz, P.E. *How to Kill a City: Gentrification, Inequality, and the Fight for the Neighborhood* (New York: Nation Books, 2018).

Myers-Lipton, Scott. *Change! A Guide to Teaching Social Action* (New York: Routledge, 2022).

Nelson, Lise, Barbara E. Smith, and Jamie Winders. "Between Aggrieved Whiteness and Class Precarity: A Feminist Politics of Interpretation," *Gender, Place, and Culture: A Journal of Feminist Geography* 29.7 (2022): 961–982.

Nusbaum, Martha. *Women and Human Development: The Capabilities Approach* (Cambridge, UK: Cambridge University Press, 2001).

Orbell, John et al. "Explaining Discussion-induced Cooperation," *Journal of Personality and Social Psychology* 54 (1988): 811–819.

Painter, Nell Irvin. *The History of White People* (New York: WW Norton, 2010).

Penner, Andrew M., and Aliya Saperstein. "Engendering Racial Perceptions: An Intersectional Analysis of How Social Status Shapes Race." *Gender and Society* 27 (2013): 319–343.

Phelan, J., B.G. Link, R.E. Moore, and A. Stueve. "The Stigma of Homelessness: The Impact of the Label 'Homeless' on Attitudes Toward Poor Persons." *Social Psychology Quarterly* 60.4 (1997): 323–337.

Plato, *Republic*. Trans. G.M.A. Grube. (Indianapolis, IN: Hackett, 1992).

Pruitt, Lisa R. "Who's Afraid of White Class Migrants? On Denial, Discrediting, and Disdain (and Toward a Richer Conception of Diversity)," *Columbia Journal of Gender and Law* 31 (2015): 196–254.

Rawls, John. *A Theory of Justice* (Cambridge, MA: Harvard University Press, 1999).

Rawls, John. *Political Liberalism* (New York: Colombia University Press, 2005).

Rich, Camille Gear. "Marginal Whiteness," *California Law Review* 98.5 (October 2010): 1497–1593.

Robinson, Cedric J. *Black Marxism: The Making of the Black Radical Tradition*. 3rd ed. (Chapel Hill: University of North Carolina Press, 2021).

Roediger, David. *The Wages of Whiteness: Race and the Making of the American Working Class*. 4th ed. (London: Verso, 2022).

Rothenberg, Paula S. *White Privilege: Readings on the Other Side of Racism*. 5th ed. (New York: Worth Publishers, 2016).

Rothstein, Richard. *The Color of Law: A Forgotten History of How Our Government Segregated America* (New York: Norton, 2018).

Santos, L., J. Voelkel, R. Willer, and J. Zaki, "Belief in the Utility of Cross-Partisan Empathy Reduces Partisan Animosity and Facilitates Persuasion," *Psychological Science* 33.9 (2022): 1557–1573.

Schwartz, Mildred A. *Trends in White Attitudes Toward Negroes* (Chicago: National Opinion Research Center, University of Chicago, 1967).

Shelby, Tommie. "Race and Social Justice: Rawlsian Considerations," *Fordham Law Review* 72.5 (2004): 1697–1714.

Shelby, Tommie. "Racial Realities and Corrective Justice: A Reply to Charles Mills," *Critical Philosophy of Race* 1.2 (2013): 145–162.

Sherman, Jeffrey W., Steven J. Stroessner, Frederica R. Conroy, and Omar A. Azam. "Prejudice and Stereotype Maintenance Processes: Attention, Attribution, and Individuation" *Journal of Personality and Social Psychology* 89.4 (2005): 607–622.

Sheth, Falguni. *Toward a Political Philosophy of Race* (Albany: SUNY Press, 2009).

Smith, David Livingstone. *The Most Dangerous Animal: Human Nature and the Origins of War* (New York: St. Martin's Press, 2007).

Smith, David Livingstone. *Less Than Human: Why We Demean, Enslave, and Exterminate Others* (New York: St. Martin's Press, 2011).

Song, Lisa, Neela Banerjee, and David Hasemyer. "Exxon Confirmed Global Warming Consensus in 1982 with In-House Climate Models," *Inside Climate News.* September 22, 2015.

Stein, Samuel. *Capital City: Gentrification and the Real Estate State* (London: Verso, 2019).

Sullivan, Shannon. *Revealing Whiteness: The Unconscious Habits of Racial Privilege* (Bloomington: Indiana University Press, 2006).

Sullivan, Shannon. *Good White People: The Problem with Middle Class Anti-Racism* (Albany, SUNY Press, 2014).

Taiwo, Olufemi. *Elite Capture: How the Powerful Took Over Identity Politics (And Everything Else)* (Chicago: Haymarket Books, 2022).

Tajfel, H. "Experiments in Intergroup Discrimination," *Scientific American* 223 (1970): 96–102.

Tajfel, H., M.G. Billig, R.P. Blundy, and Claude Flament. "Social Categorization and Intergroup Behavior," *European Journal of Social Psychology* 1.2 (1971): 149–177.

The Combahee River Collective. "The Combahee River Collective Statement," in *Home Girls, A Black Feminist Anthology,* ed. Barbara Smith (Rutgers, NJ: Rutgers University Press, 2000).

Tilly, Charles. *Durable Inequality* (Berkeley: University of California Press, 1998).

Ture, Kwame (formerly Stokely Carmichael), and Charles Hamilton. *Black Power: The Politics of Liberation* (New York: Vintage, 1992).

Union of Concerned Scientists. *Smoke, Mirrors & Hot Air: How ExxonMobil Uses Big Tobacco's Tactics to Manufacture Uncertainty on Climate Science* (Cambridge, MA: Union of Concerned Scientists, 2007).

Zack, Naomi. *White Privilege and Black Rights: The Injustice of U.S. Police Racial Profiling and Homicide* (Lanham, MD: Rowman and Littlefield, 2015).

INDEX

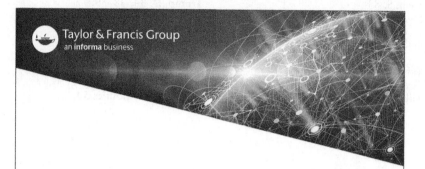

Made in United States
North Haven, CT
04 February 2025

65374375R00076